IRELAND

PHOTOGRAPHS BY Tom Kelly

Catalog No. V216
Published by Pomegranate Communications, Inc.
Box 808022, Petaluma CA 94975

Available in Canada from Canadian Manda Group
165 Dufferin Street, Toronto, Ontario M6K 3H6

Available in the UK and mainland Europe from Pomegranate Europe Ltd.
Unit 1, Heathcote Business Centre, Hurlbutt Road, Warwick, Warwickshire CV34 6TD, UK

Available in Australia from Hardie Grant Books, 12 Claremont Street, South Yarra, Victoria 3141

Available in New Zealand from Southern Publishers Group, P.O. Box 8360, Symonds Street, Auckland

Available in the Far East from Julian Ashton, Ashton International Marketing Services
P.O. Box 298, Sevenoaks, Kent TN13 1WU, UK

Africa, Latin America, and the Middle East: info@pomegranate.com; 707-782-9000

Pomegranate also publishes Tom Kelly's work in a 2007 wall calendar, a deluxe address book, notecards and boxed panoramic notecards, magnets, and bookmarks. Our products and publications include many other calendars in several formats, books, posters, postcards and books of postcards, magnets, mousepads, Knowledge Cards®, birthday books, journals, jigsaw puzzles, designer gift wrap, and stationery sets. For more information or to place an order, please contact Pomegranate Communications, Inc.:
800-227-1428; www.pomegranate.com.

Cover image: Flowery Wellington boots

Designed by Ronni Madrid

Dates in color indicate federal holidays.
All astronomical data supplied in this calendar are expressed in Greenwich Mean Time (GMT).

● NEW MOON   ☽ FIRST QUARTER   ○ FULL MOON   ☾ LAST QUARTER

2007 ENGAGEMENT CALENDAR

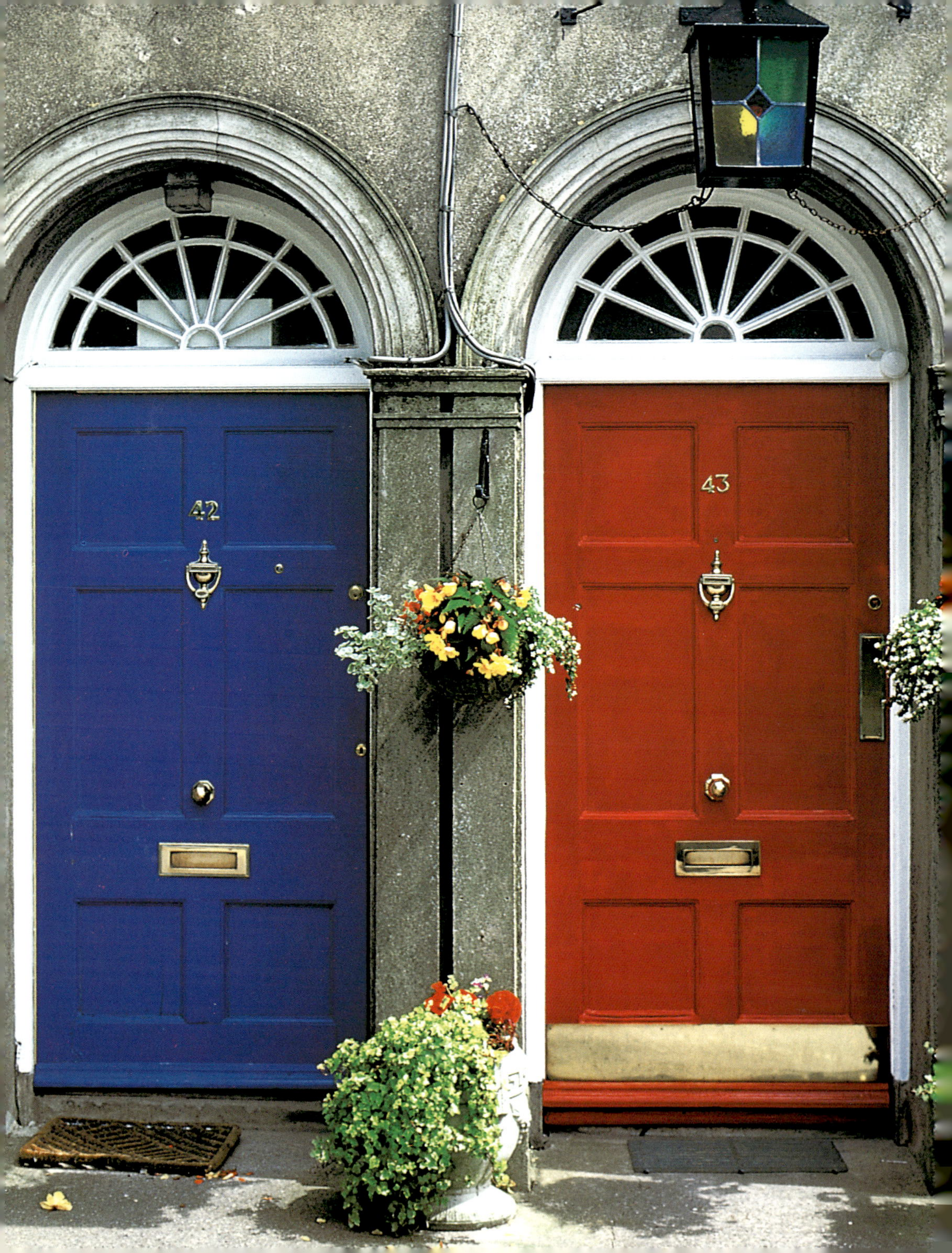
42
43

JANUARY

Poor nations are hungry, and rich nations are proud; and pride and hunger will ever be at variance.
—Jonathan Swift (1667–1745)

NEW YEAR'S DAY | *monday*

1 1

BANK HOLIDAY (SCOTLAND) | *tuesday*

2 2

wednesday

○ **3** 3

thursday

4 4

friday

5 5

KINSALE, COUNTY CORK

saturday

6 6

s	m	t	w	t	f	s
	1	2	3	4	5	6
7	8	9	10	11	12	13
14	15	16	17	18	19	20
21	22	23	24	25	26	27
28	29	30	31			

JANUARY

sunday

7 7

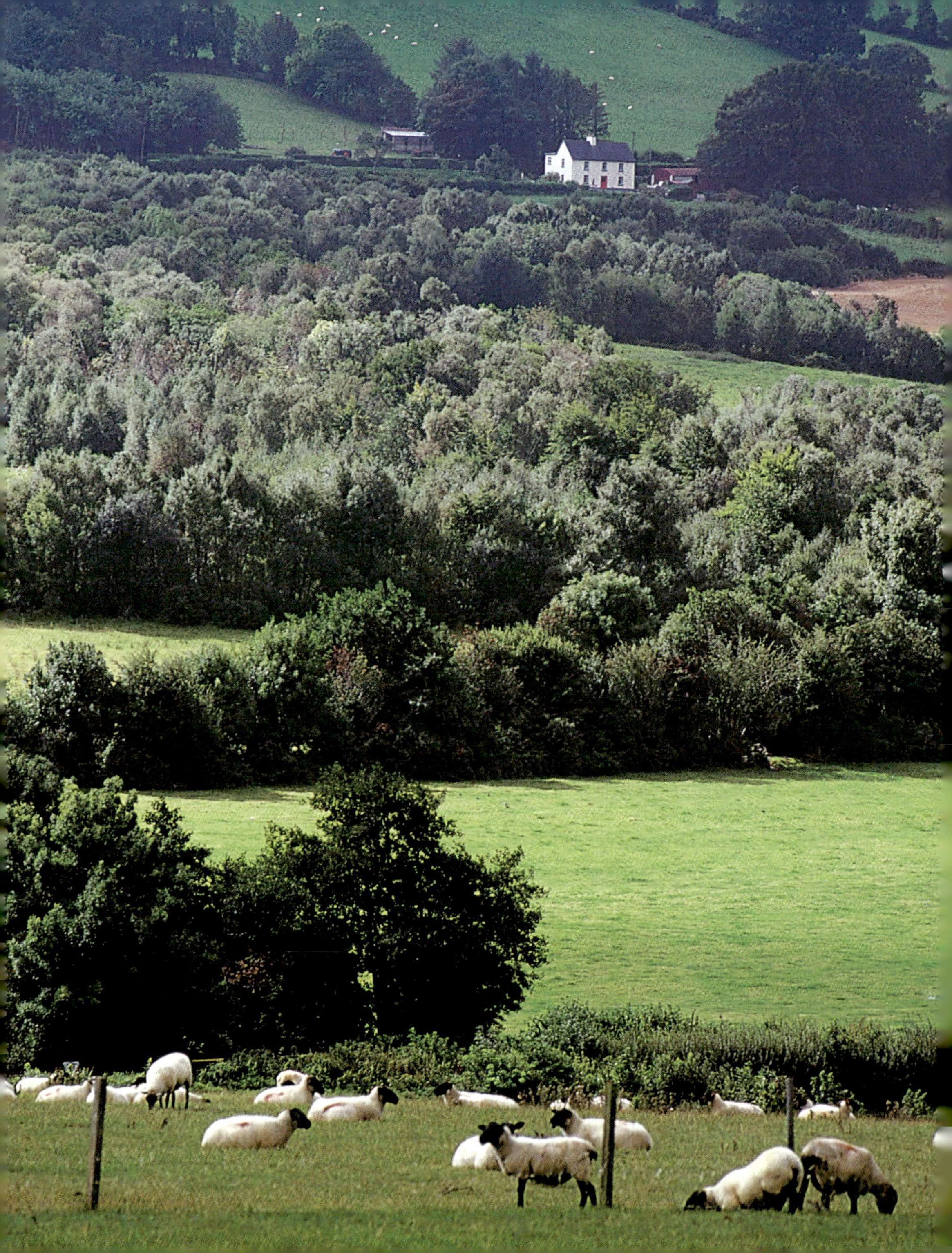

O bear me my blessing afar to the West,
For the heart in my bosom is broken; I fail.
Should death of a sudden now pierce my breast
I should die of the love that I bear the Gael!
　　　　—St. Columcille (521–576)

LEMYBRIEN, COUNTY WATERFORD

s	m	t	w	t	f	s
	1	2	3	4	5	6
7	8	9	10	11	12	13
14	15	16	17	18	19	20
21	22	23	24	25	26	27
28	29	30	31			

JANUARY

monday
8 8

tuesday
9 9

wednesday
10 10

thursday
☾ **11** 11

friday
12 12

saturday
13 13

sunday
14 14

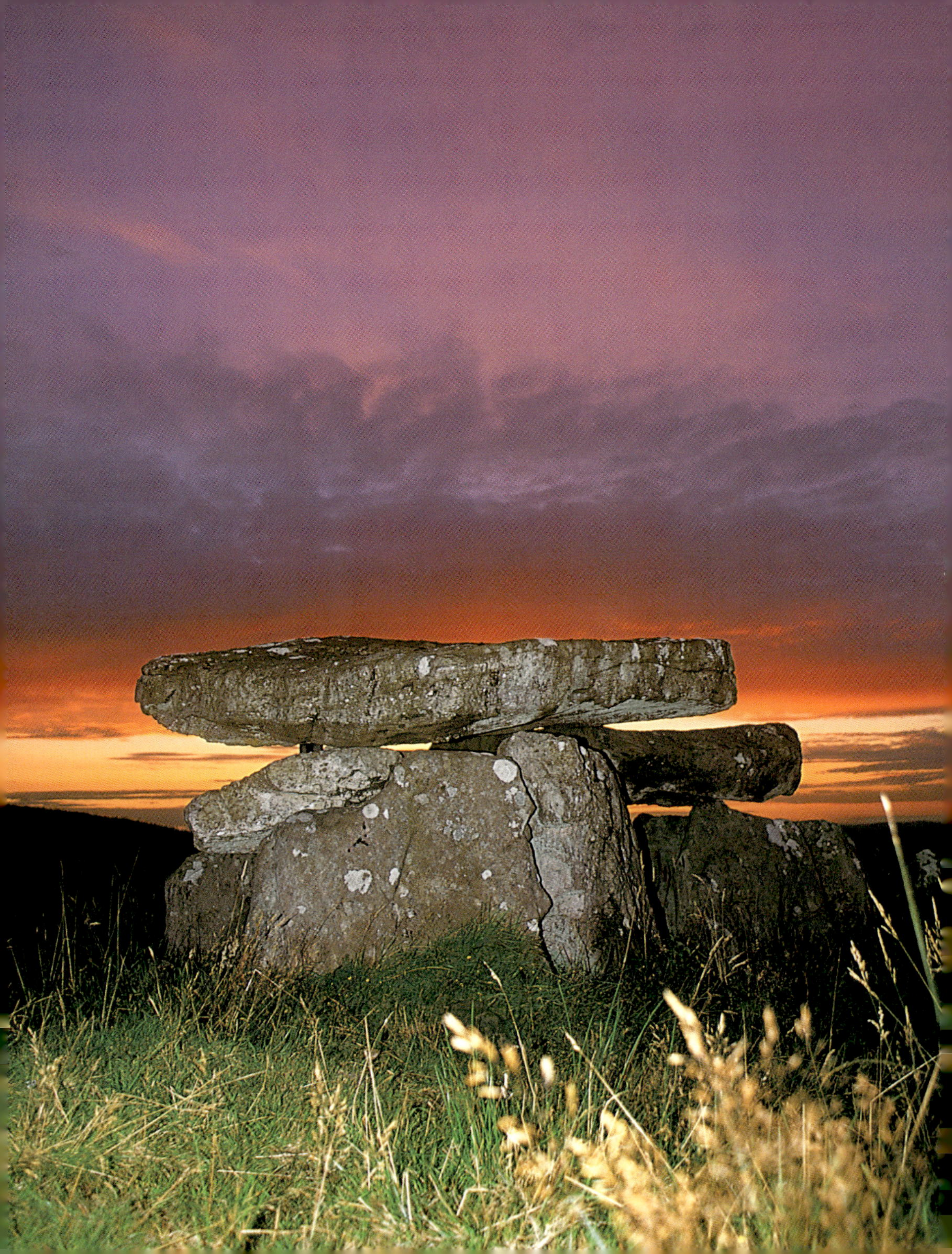

*T*he tears of the world are a con-
stant quality. For each one who
begins to weep, somewhere else
another stops. The same is true of
the laugh.
— Samuel Beckett (1906–1989)

monday

15 15

tuesday

16 16

wednesday

17 17

thursday

18 18

friday

● **19** 19

DUNTRYLEAGUE PASSAGE GRAVE,
COUNTY LIMERICK

saturday

20 20

s	m	t	w	t	f	s
	1	2	3	4	5	6
7	8	9	10	11	12	13
14	15	16	17	18	19	20
21	22	23	24	25	26	27
28	29	30	31			

JANUARY

sunday

21 21

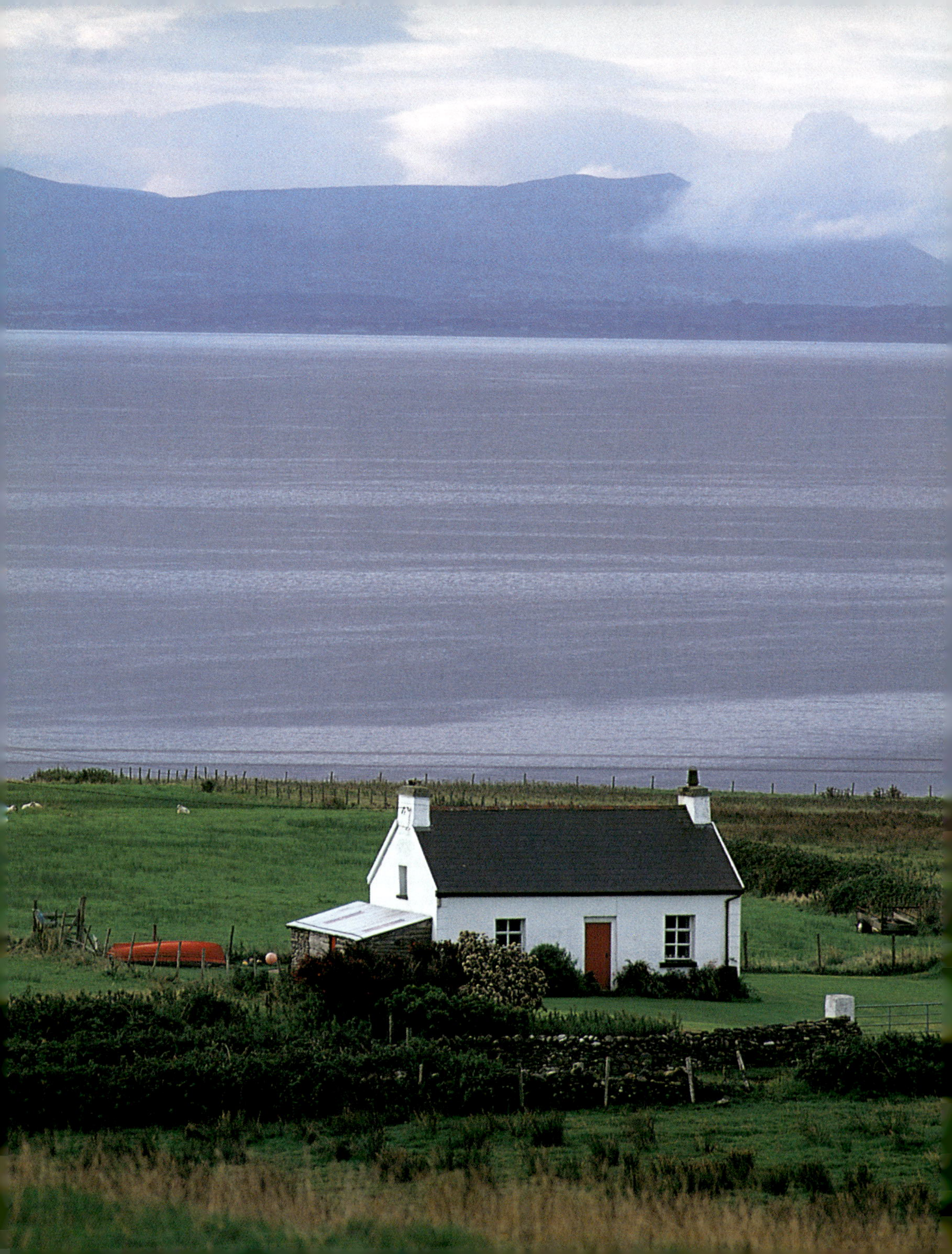

*T*his I dare avow: there are more rivers, lakes, brooks, strands, quagmires, bogs, and marshes in this country than in all Christendom besides. In five months' space I quite spoiled six horses, and myself as tired as the worst of them.
—William Lithgow (1582–1645)

MCSWYNE'S BAY,
COUNTY DONEGAL

s	m	t	w	t	f	s
	1	2	3	4	5	6
7	8	9	10	11	12	13
14	15	16	17	18	19	20
21	22	23	24	25	26	27
28	29	30	31			

monday
22 22

tuesday
23 23

wednesday
24 24

thursday
☽ **25** 25

friday
26 26

saturday
27 27

sunday
28 28

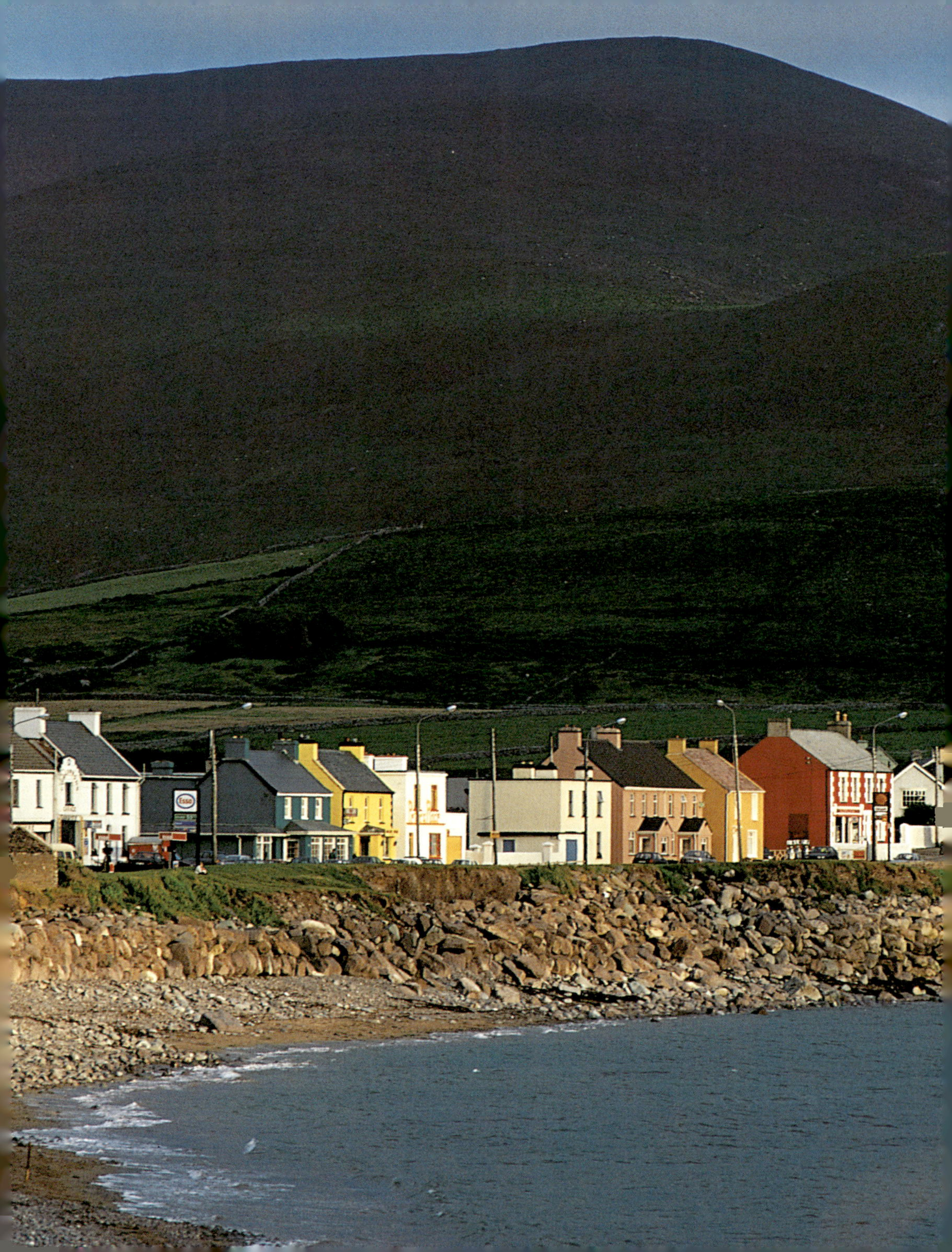
Esso

*W*hen I came back to Dublin I
was court-martialled in my
absence and sentenced to death in
my absence, so I said they could
shoot me in my absence.
—Brendan Behan (1923–1964)

monday

29 29

tuesday

30 30

wednesday

31 31

thursday

1 32

friday

○ **2** 33

WATERVILLE, COUNTY KERRY

saturday

3 34

s	m	t	w	t	f	s
				1	2	3
4	5	6	7	8	9	10
11	12	13	14	15	16	17
18	19	20	21	22	23	24
25	26	27	28			

FEBRUARY

sunday

4 35

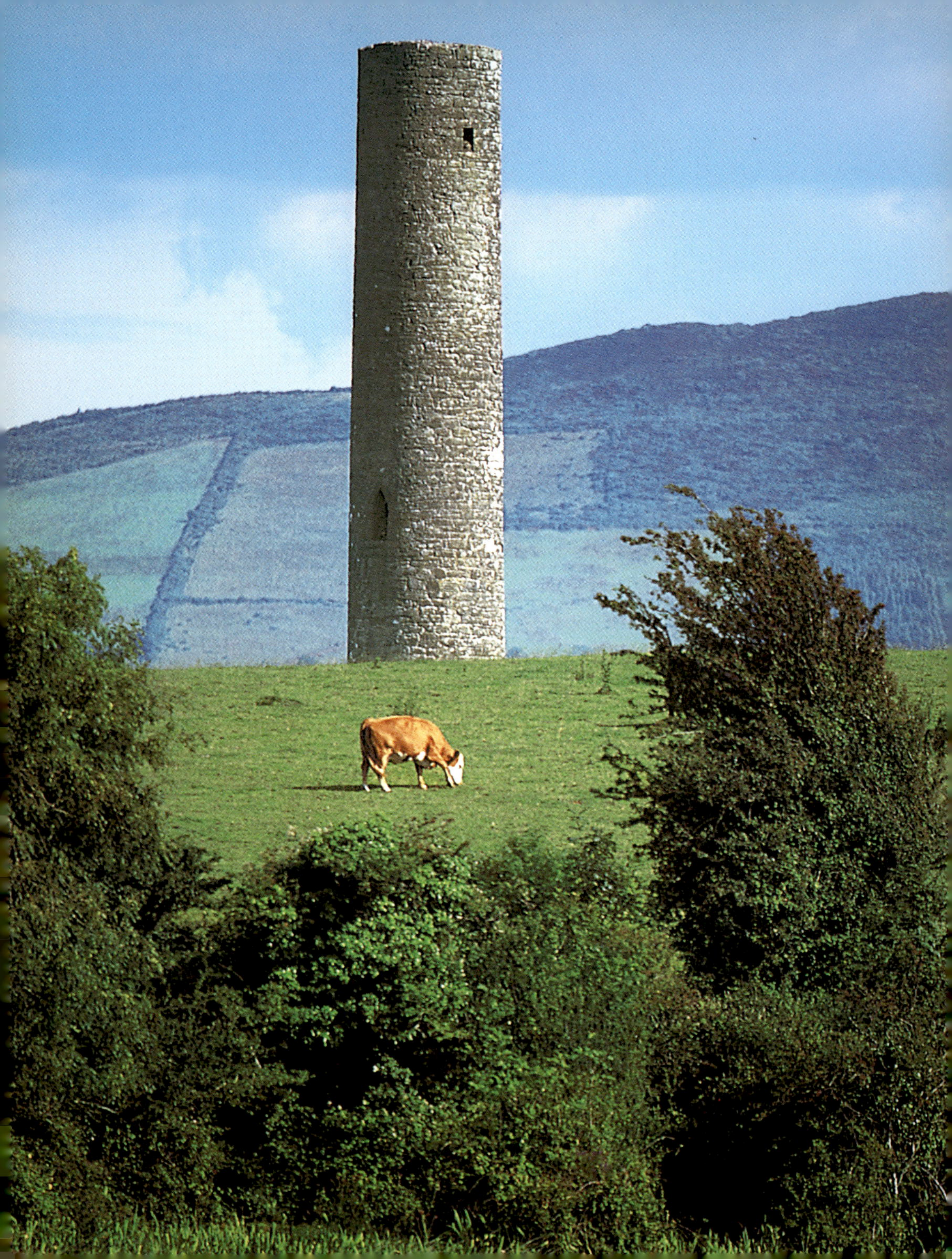

T here are some faults so nearly allied to excellence that we can scarce weed out the vice without eradicating the virtue.
—Oliver Goldsmith (1730–1774)

monday

5 36

tuesday

6 37

wednesday

7 38

thursday

8 39

friday

9 40

HOLY ISLAND, COUNTY CLARE

saturday

☾ 10 41

s	m	t	w	t	f	s
				1	2	3
4	5	6	7	8	9	10
11	12	13	14	15	16	17
18	19	20	21	22	23	24
25	26	27	28			

FEBRUARY

sunday

11 42

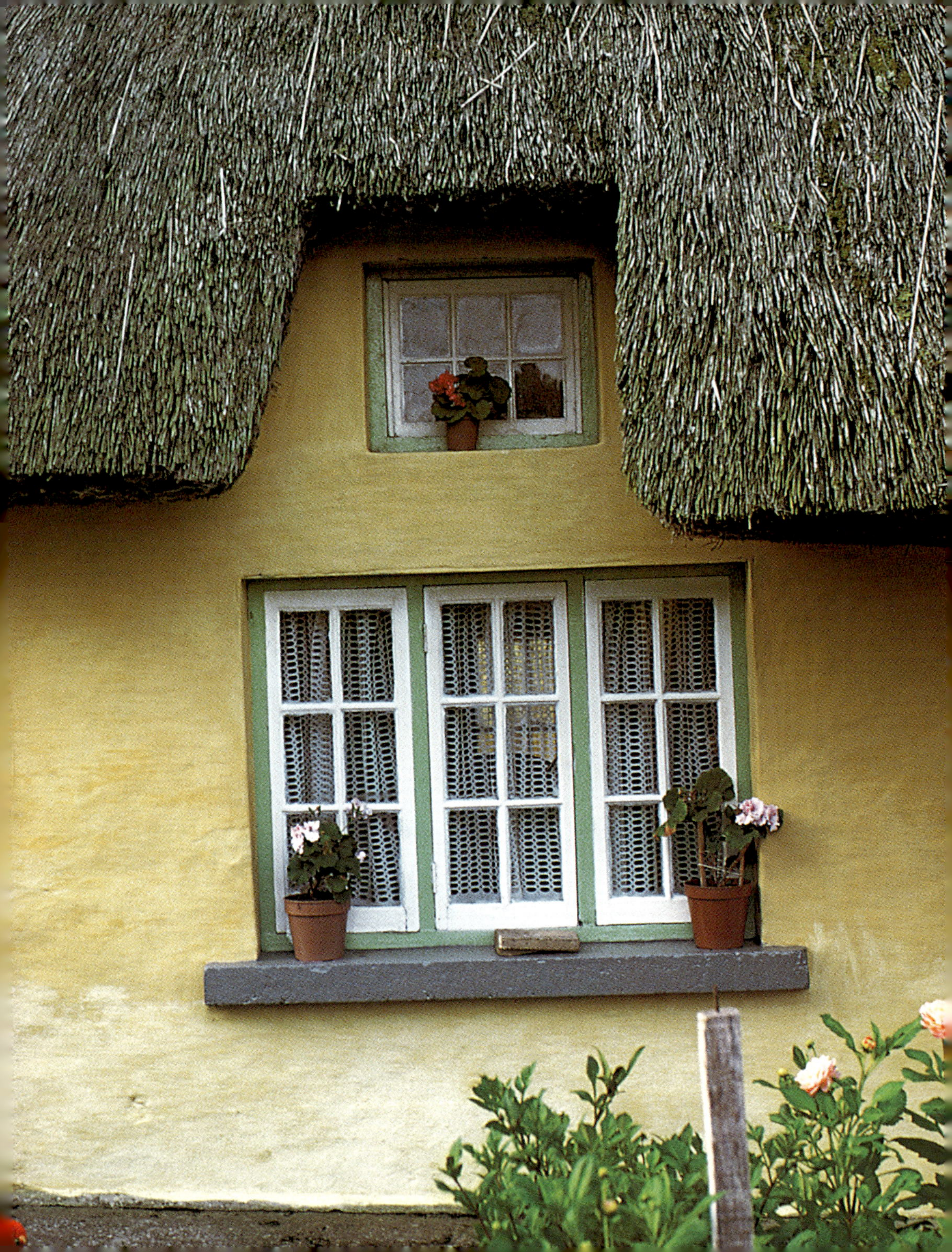

l love everything that's old: old friends, old times, old manners, old books, old wines; and, I believe, Dorothy, you'll own I have been pretty fond of an old wife.
—Oliver Goldsmith (1730–1774)

LINCOLN'S BIRTHDAY

monday

12 43

tuesday

13 44

VALENTINE'S DAY

wednesday

14 45

thursday

15 46

friday

16 47

ADARE, COUNTY LIMERICK

saturday

17 48

s	m	t	w	t	f	s
				1	2	3
4	5	6	7	8	9	10
11	12	13	14	15	16	17
18	19	20	21	22	23	24
25	26	27	28			

FEBRUARY

sunday

18 49

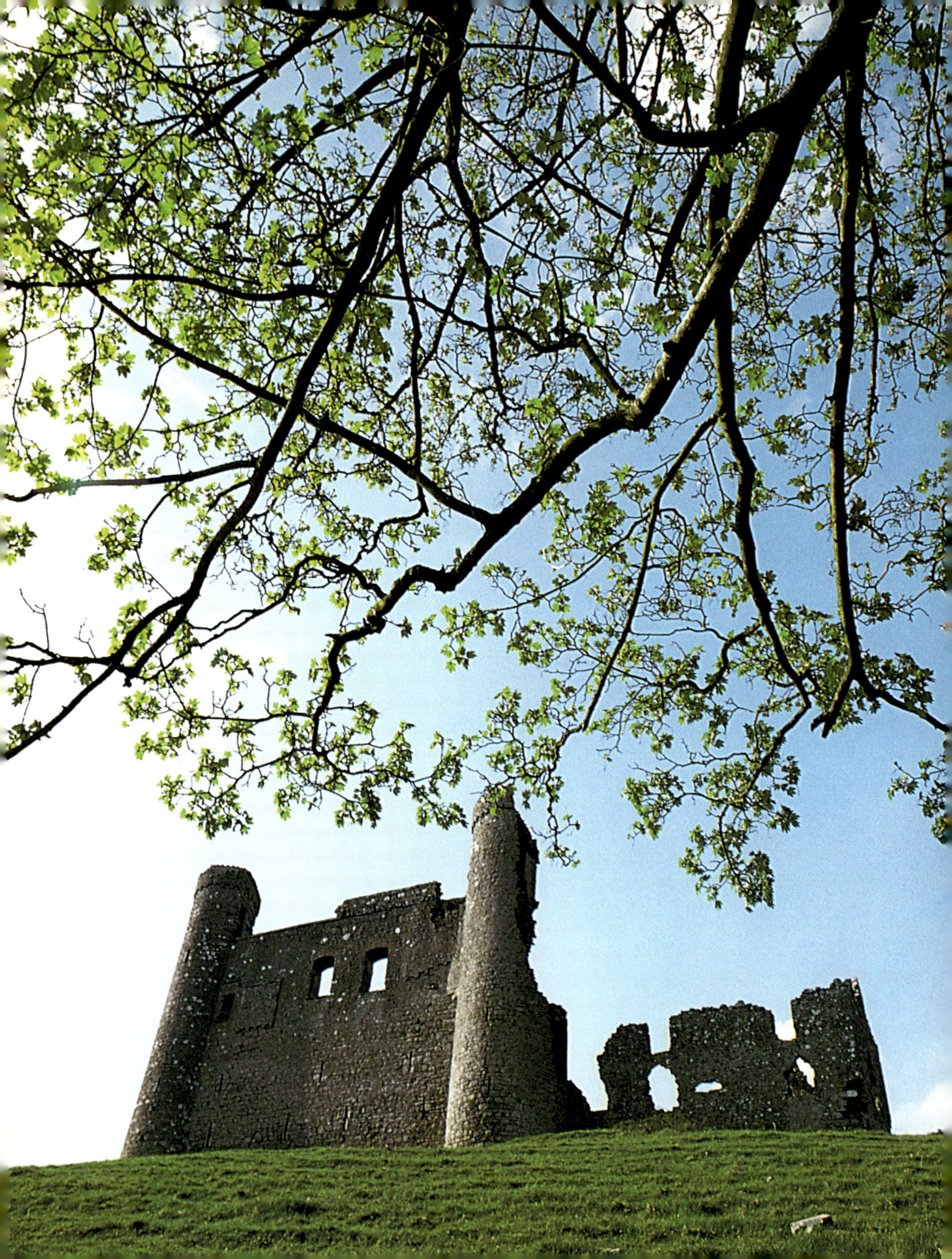

Newspapers are unable, seemingly, to discriminate between a bicycle accident and the collapse of civilisation.

—George Bernard Shaw
(1856–1950)

PRESIDENTS' DAY

monday

19 50

tuesday

20 51

ASH WEDNESDAY

wednesday

21 52

WASHINGTON'S BIRTHDAY

thursday

22 53

friday

23 54

DUNMOE CASTLE, COUNTY MEATH

saturday

☽ **24** 55

s	m	t	w	t	f	s
				1	2	3
4	5	6	7	8	9	10
11	12	13	14	15	16	17
18	19	20	21	22	23	24
25	26	27	28			

FEBRUARY

sunday

25 56

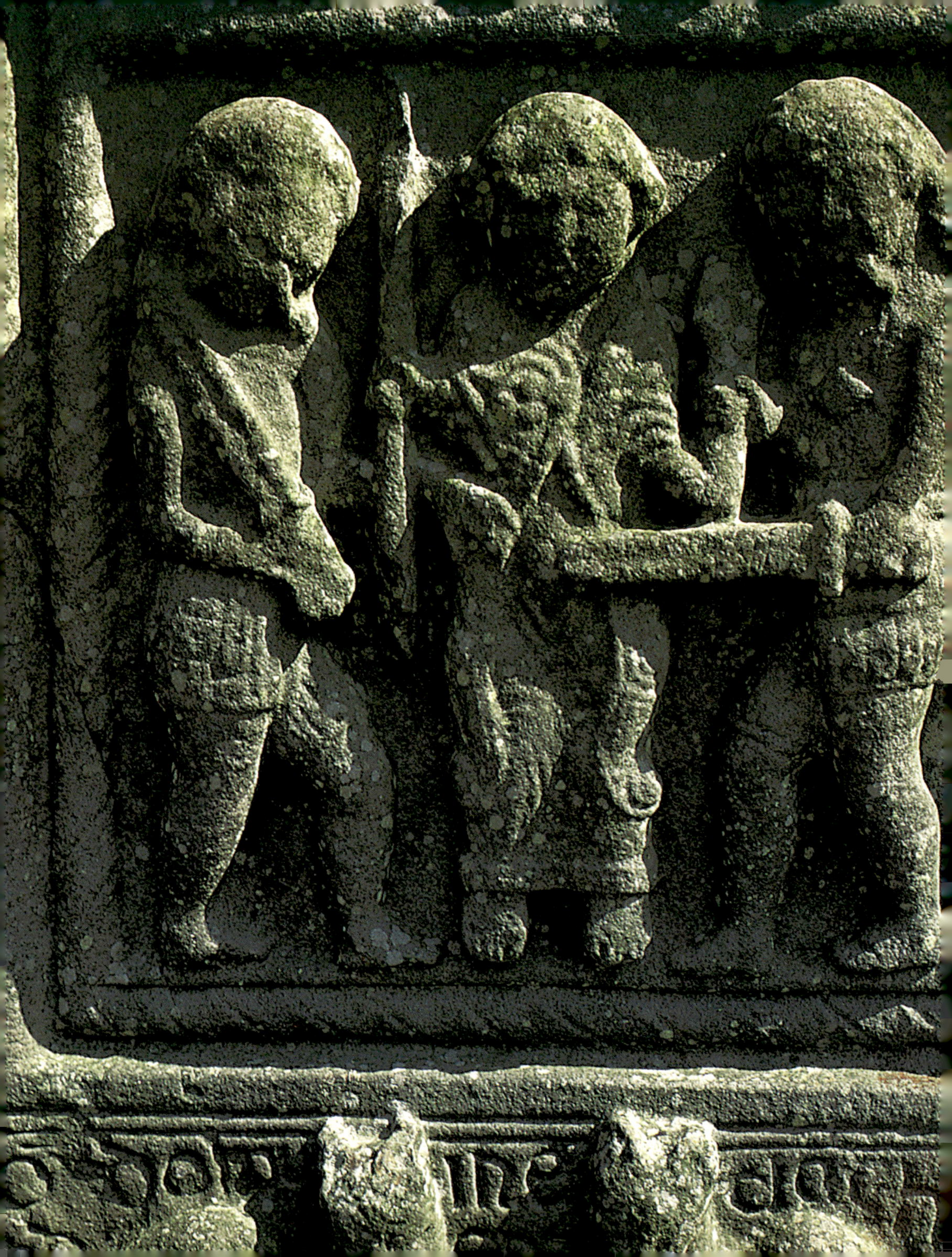

The wrong way always seems the more reasonable.
—George Moore (1852–1933)

26 57

27 58

28 59

1 60

2 61

MUIREDACH'S CROSS,
MONASTERBOICE, COUNTY LOUTH

PURIM (BEGINS AT SUNSET)
3 62

s	m	t	w	t	f	s
				1	2	3
4	5	6	7	8	9	10
11	12	13	14	15	16	17
18	19	20	21	22	23	24
25	26	27	28	29	30	31

MARCH

4 63

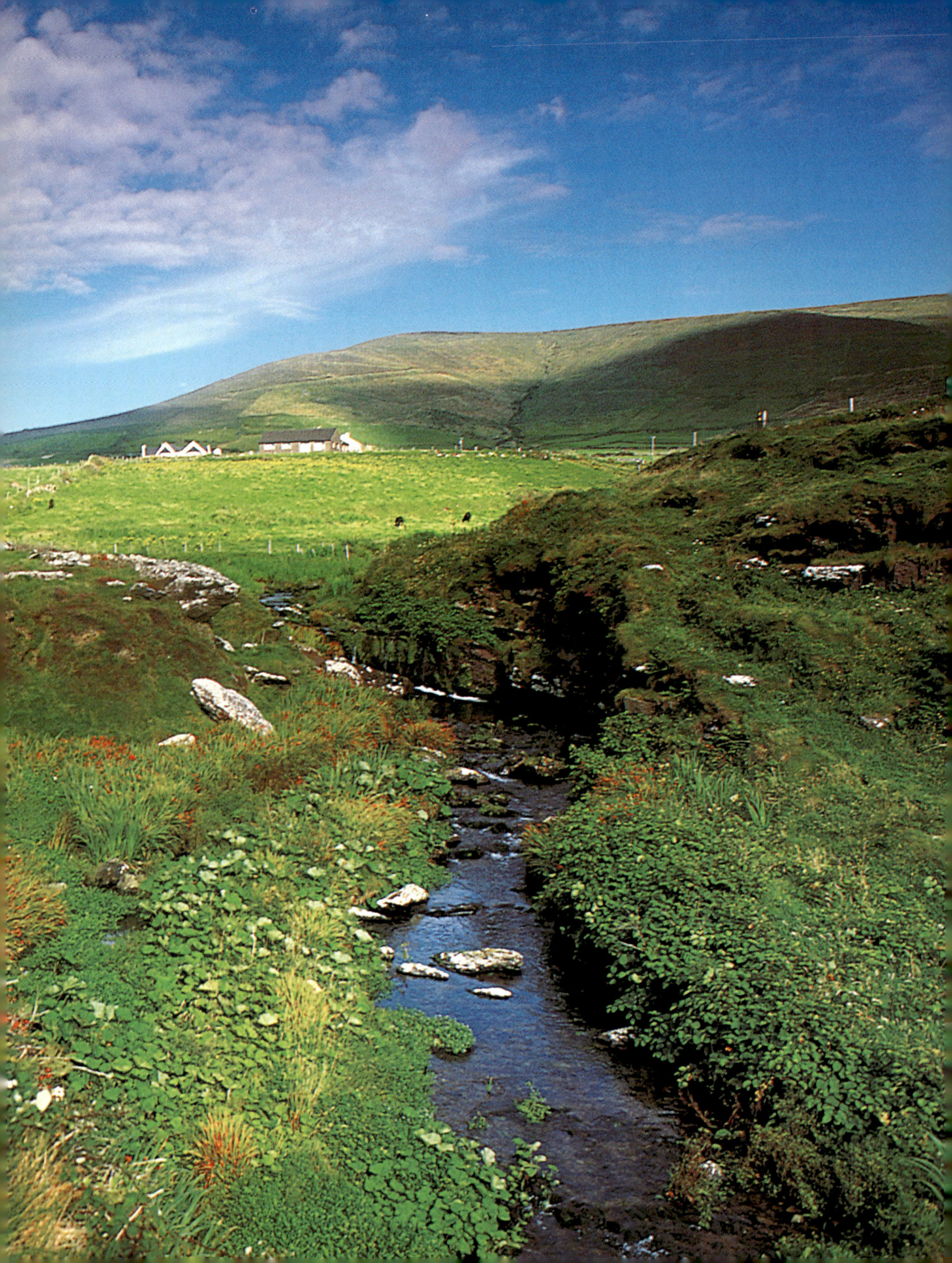

*I*t's a good thing to be able to take up your money in your hand and to think no more of it when it slips away from you than you would of a trout that would slip back into the stream.

—Lady Gregory (1852–1932)

monday

5 ₆₄

tuesday

6 ₆₅

wednesday

7 ₆₆

INTERNATIONAL WOMEN'S DAY   *thursday*

8 ₆₇

friday

9 ₆₈

THREE SISTERS HEAD,
COUNTY KERRY

saturday

10 ₆₉

s	m	t	w	t	f	s
				1	2	3
4	5	6	7	8	9	10
11	12	13	14	15	16	17
18	19	20	21	22	23	24
25	26	27	28	29	30	31

MARCH

DAYLIGHT SAVING TIME BEGINS   *sunday*

11 ₇₀

I can resist everything except temptation.
—Oscar Wilde (1854–1900)

monday

☾ **12** 71

tuesday

13 72

wednesday

14 73

thursday

15 74

friday

16 75

ROSS CARBERY, COUNTY CORK

ST. PATRICK'S DAY   *saturday*

17 76

s	m	t	w	t	f	s
				1	2	3
4	5	6	7	8	9	10
11	12	13	14	15	16	17
18	19	20	21	22	23	24
25	26	27	28	29	30	31

MARCH

MOTHERING SUNDAY (UK)   *sunday*

18 77

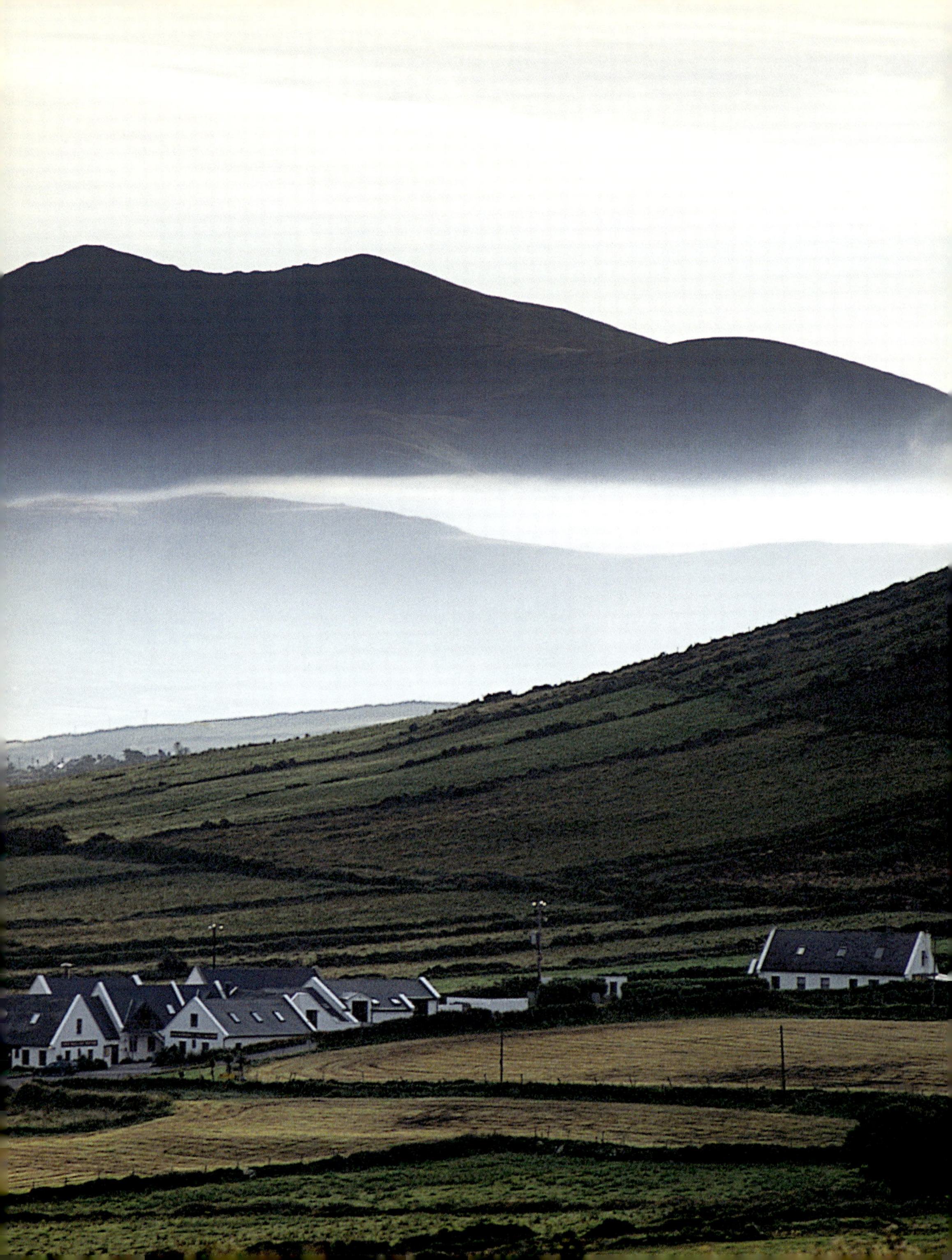

*H*umans are amphibians—half spirit and half animal.... As spirits they belong to the eternal world, but as animals they inhabit time.

—C. S. Lewis (1898–1963)

monday

● **19** 78

tuesday

20 79

VERNAL EQUINOX 12:07 AM (GMT)

wednesday

21 80

thursday

22 81

friday

23 82

VENTRY HARBOUR, COUNTY KERRY

saturday

24 83

s	m	t	w	t	f	s
				1	2	3
4	5	6	7	8	9	10
11	12	13	14	15	16	17
18	19	20	21	22	23	24
25	26	27	28	29	30	31

MARCH

SUMMER TIME BEGINS (UK)

sunday

☽ **25** 84

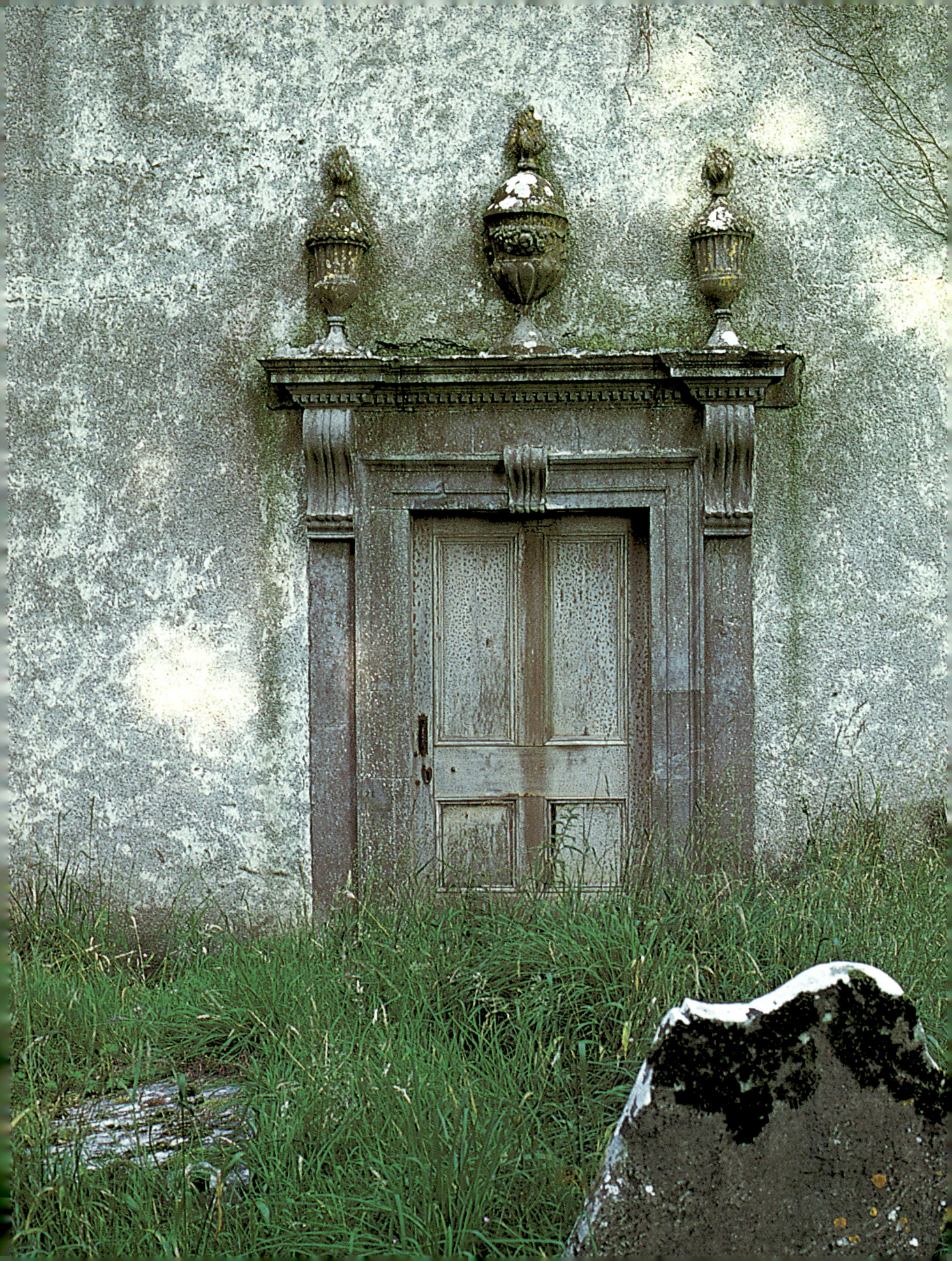

*P*ersonally I have no bone to pick
with graveyards, I take the air
there willingly, perhaps more willingly than elsewhere, when take the
air I must.
—Samuel Beckett (1906–1989)

DURROW, COUNTY OFFALY

s	m	t	w	t	f	s
1	2	3	4	5	6	7
8	9	10	11	12	13	14
15	16	17	18	19	20	21
22	23	24	25	26	27	28
29	30					

APRIL

monday
26 85

tuesday
27 86

wednesday
28 87

thursday
29 88

friday
30 89

saturday
31 90

PALM SUNDAY

sunday
1 91

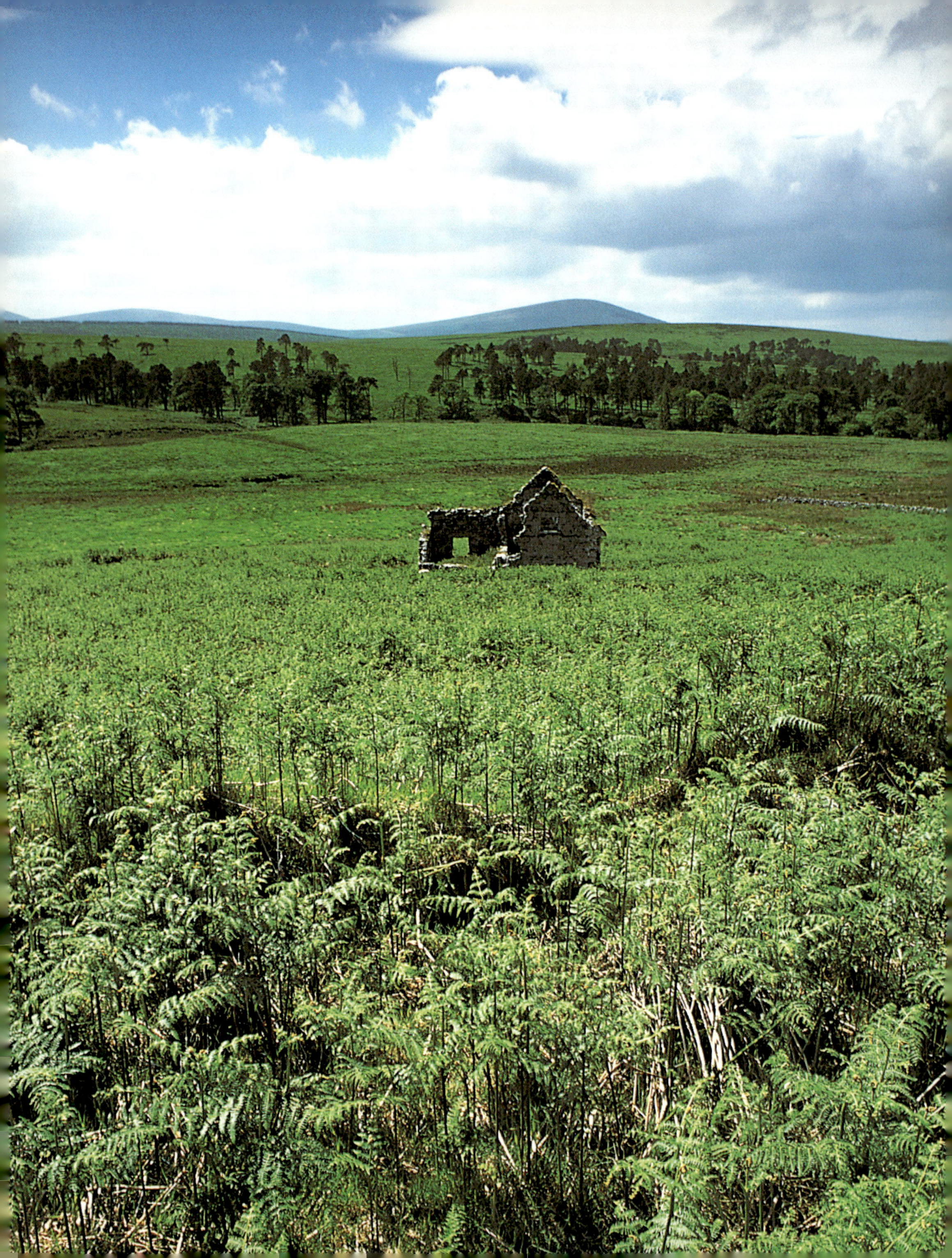

APRIL

The charm, one might say the genius of memory, is that it is choosy, chancy, and temperamental: it rejects the edifying cathedral and indelibly photographs the small boy outside, chewing a hunk of melon in the dust.

—Elizabeth Bowen (1899–1973)

PASSOVER (BEGINS AT SUNSET)

monday

2 92

tuesday

3 93

wednesday

4 94

thursday

5 95

GOOD FRIDAY

friday

6 96

RUIN, COUNTY WICKLOW

saturday

7 97

s	m	t	w	t	f	s
1	2	3	4	5	6	7
8	9	10	11	12	13	14
15	16	17	18	19	20	21
22	23	24	25	26	27	28
29	30					

APRIL

EASTER SUNDAY

sunday

8 98

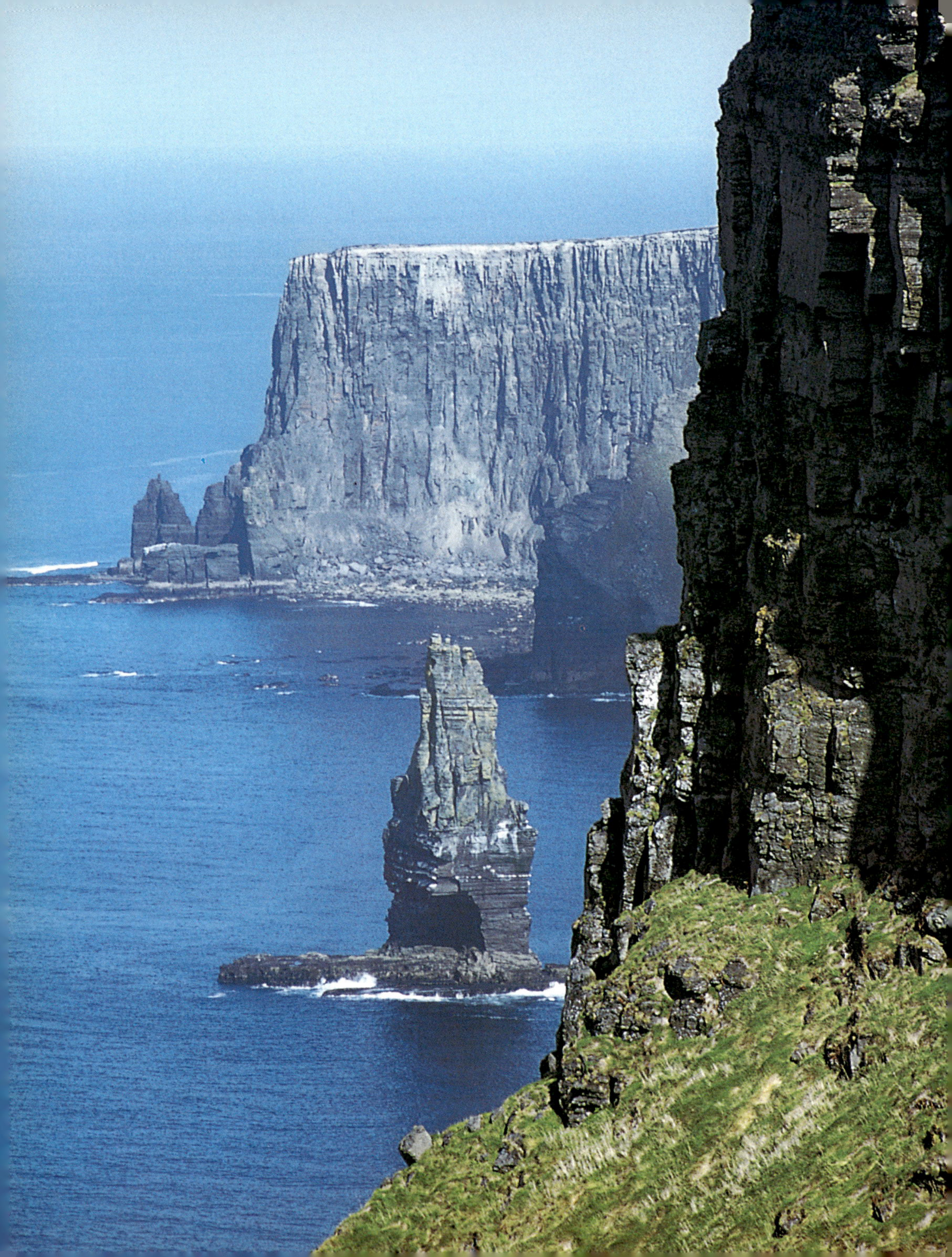

*H*ell is paved with good inten-
tions, not with bad ones. All
men mean well.
—George Bernard Shaw
(1856–1950)

monday

9 99

tuesday

☾ **10** 100

wednesday

11 101

thursday

12 102

friday

13 103

CLIFFS OF MOHER, COUNTY CLARE

saturday

14 104

sunday

15 105

s	m	t	w	t	f	s
1	2	3	4	5	6	7
8	9	10	11	12	13	14
15	16	17	18	19	20	21
22	23	24	25	26	27	28
29	30					

APRIL

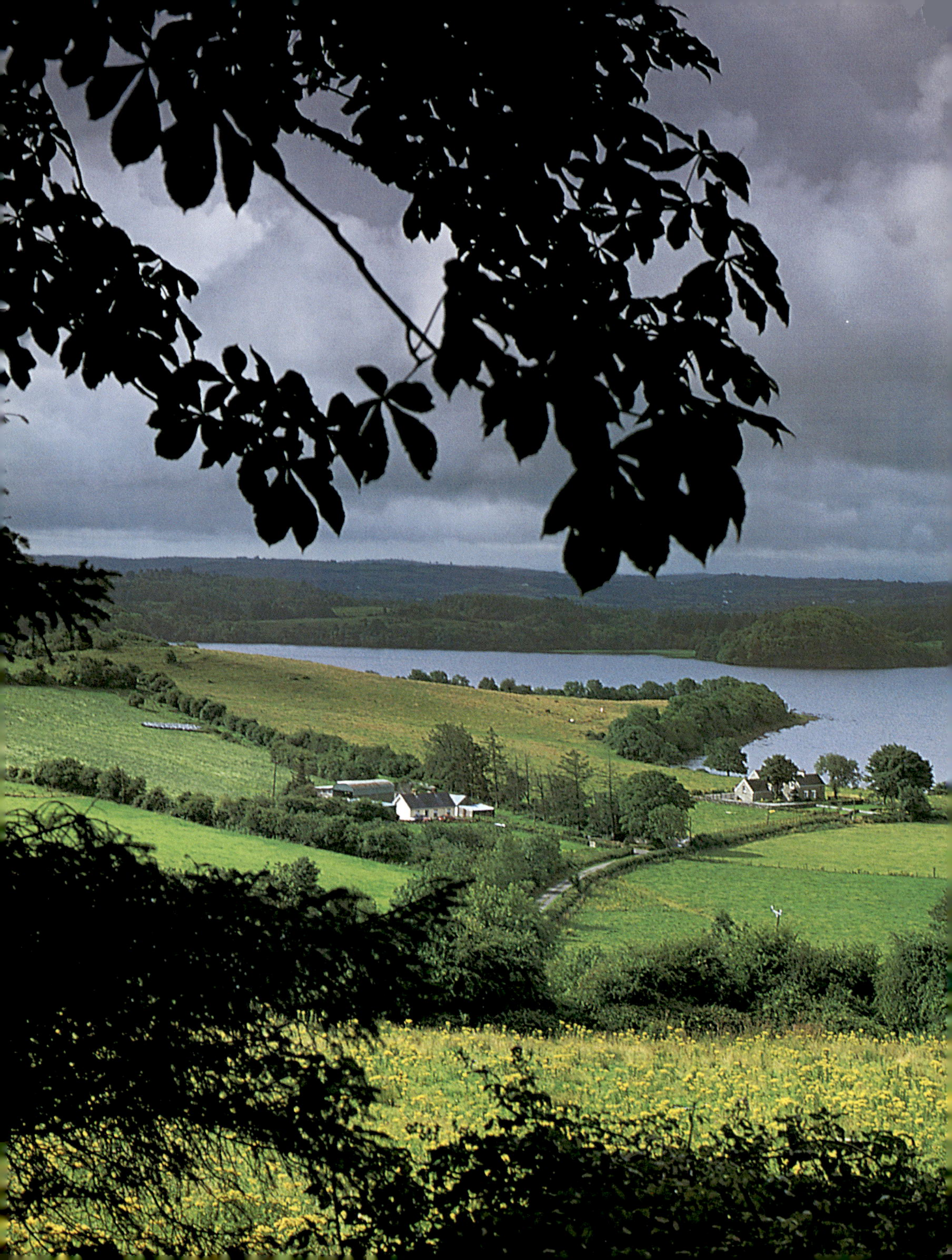

[T]he trees in Stephen's Green were fragrant of rain and the rainsodden earth gave forth its mortal odour.

—James Joyce (1882–1941)

monday
16 106

tuesday
17 107

wednesday
18 108

thursday
19 109

friday
20 110

LOUGH GILL, COUNTY SLIGO

saturday
21 111

s	m	t	w	t	f	s
1	2	3	4	5	6	7
8	9	10	11	12	13	14
15	16	17	18	19	20	21
22	23	24	25	26	27	28
29	30					

APRIL

EARTH DAY

sunday
22 112

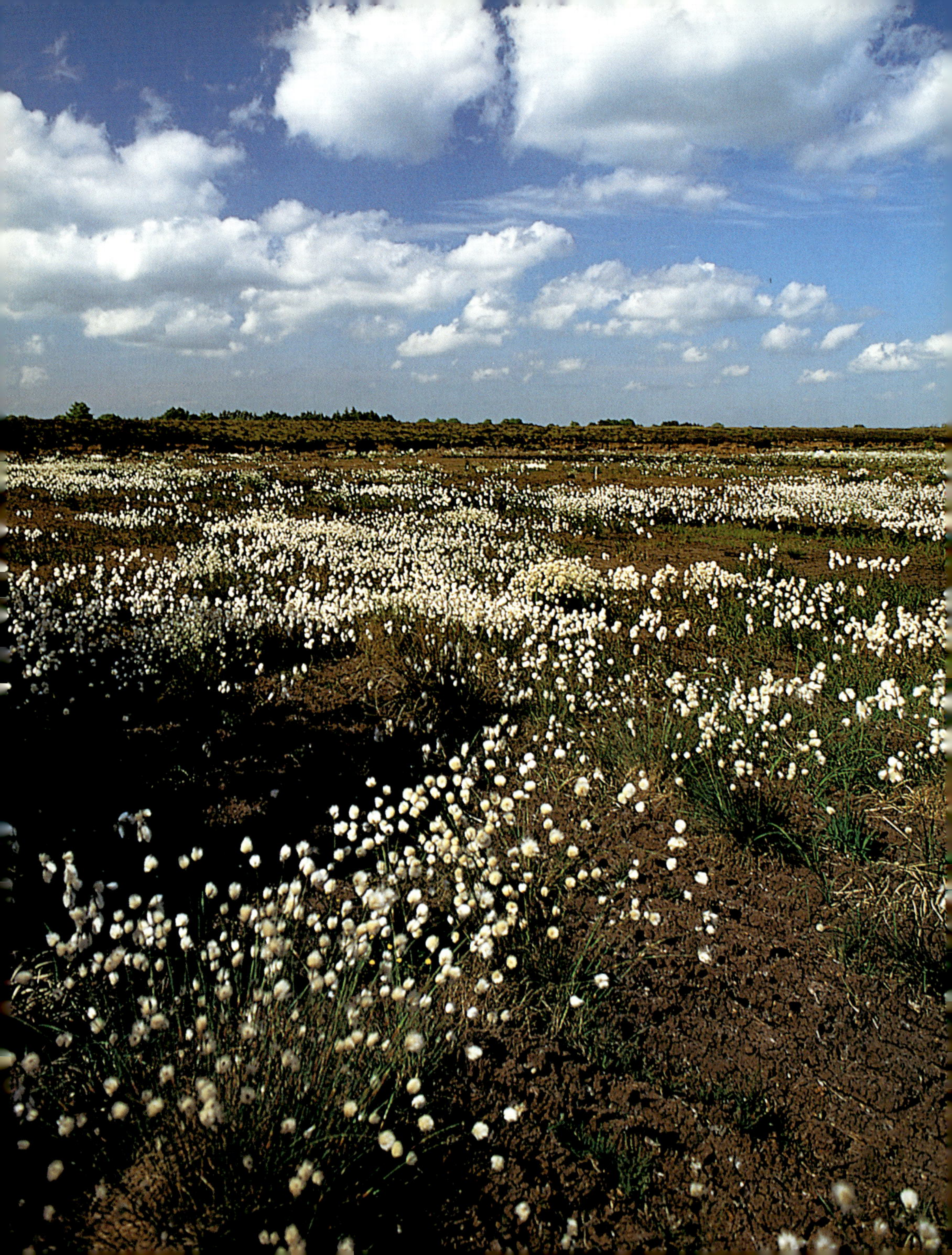

l *pedalled on towards Athlone*
through slashing rain across
brown miles of harvested bog—
looking like a child's dream of a
world made of chocolate.
 —Dervla Murphy (b. 1931)

monday

23 · 113

tuesday

☽ **24** · 114

wednesday

25 · 115

thursday

26 · 116

friday

27 · 117

BOG COTTON,
COUNTY ROSCOMMON

saturday

28 · 118

s	m	t	w	t	f	s
1	2	3	4	5	6	7
8	9	10	11	12	13	14
15	16	17	18	19	20	21
22	23	24	25	26	27	28
29	30					

sunday

29 · 119

APRIL

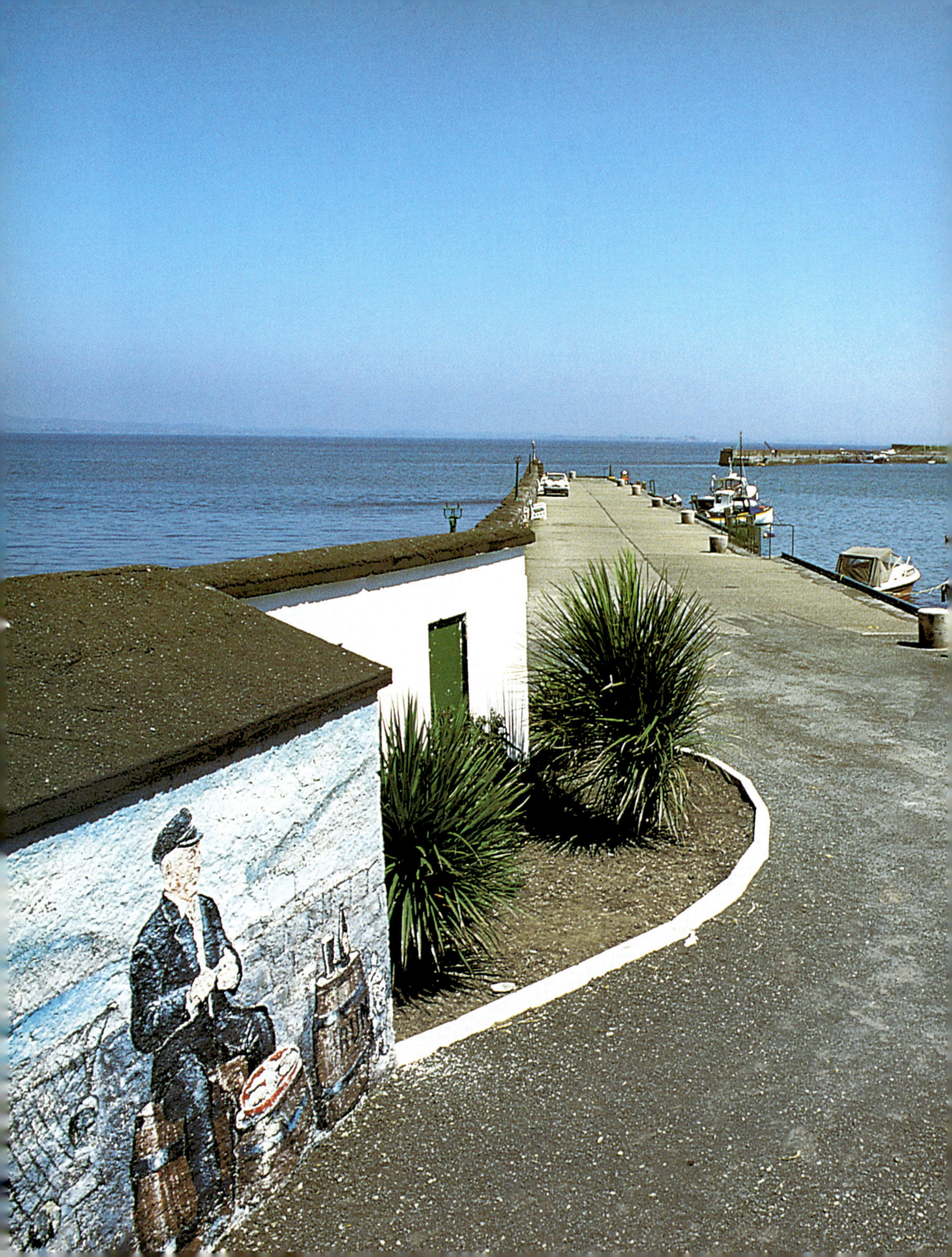

A footman may swear; but he cannot swear like a lord. He can swear as often: but can he swear with equal delicacy, propriety, and judgment?
—Jonathan Swift (1667–1745)

monday

30 120

tuesday

1 121

wednesday

2 122

thursday

3 123

friday

4 124

CARLINGFORD, COUNTY LOUTH

CINCO DE MAYO *saturday*

5 125

s	m	t	w	t	f	s
		1	2	3	4	5
6	7	8	9	10	11	12
13	14	15	16	17	18	19
20	21	22	23	24	25	26
27	28	29	30	31		

MAY

sunday

6 126

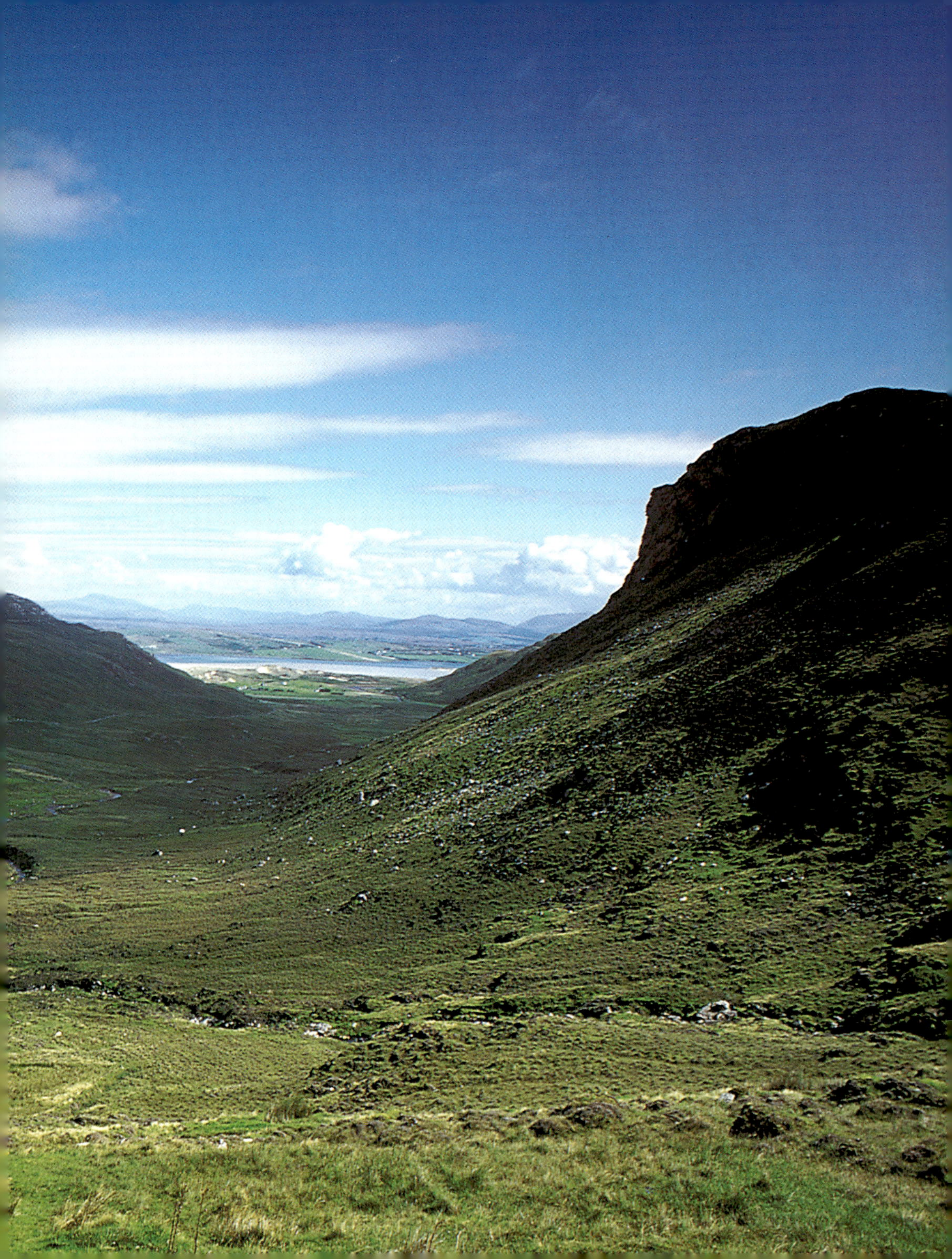

*There is not in the wide world
a valley so sweet
As that vale in whose bosom the
bright waters meet;
O the last rays of feeling and life
must depart,
Ere the bloom of that valley shall
fade from my heart.*
—Thomas Moore (1779–1852)

LOUGHROS BEG BAY,
COUNTY DONEGAL

s	m	t	w	t	f	s
		1	2	3	4	5
6	7	8	9	10	11	12
13	14	15	16	17	18	19
20	21	22	23	24	25	26
27	28	29	30	31		

MAY

BANK HOLIDAY (UK)

monday

7 127

tuesday

8 128

wednesday

9 129

thursday

☾ 10 130

friday

11 131

saturday

12 132

MOTHER'S DAY

sunday

13 133

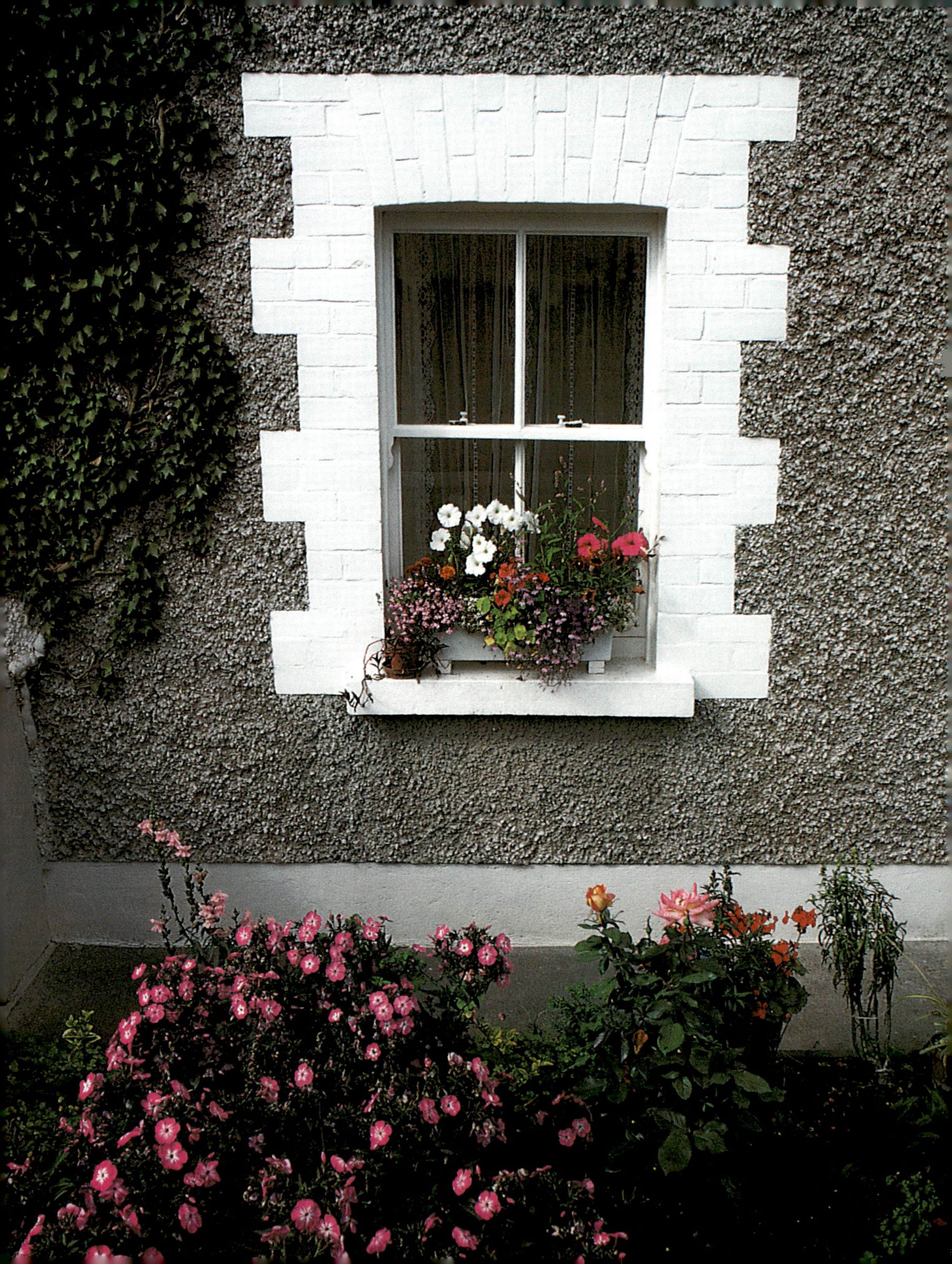

*O*á gcaillfí an Ghaeilge chaillfí
Éire. [If the Irish language were
to be lost, Ireland would perish.]
—Patrick Pearse (1879–1916)

monday
14 134

tuesday
15 135

wednesday
● ## 16 136

thursday
17 137

friday
18 138

RATHDOWNEY, COUNTY LAOIS

ARMED FORCES DAY

saturday
19 139

s	m	t	w	t	f	s
		1	2	3	4	5
6	7	8	9	10	11	12
13	14	15	16	17	18	19
20	21	22	23	24	25	26
27	28	29	30	31		

MAY

sunday
20 140

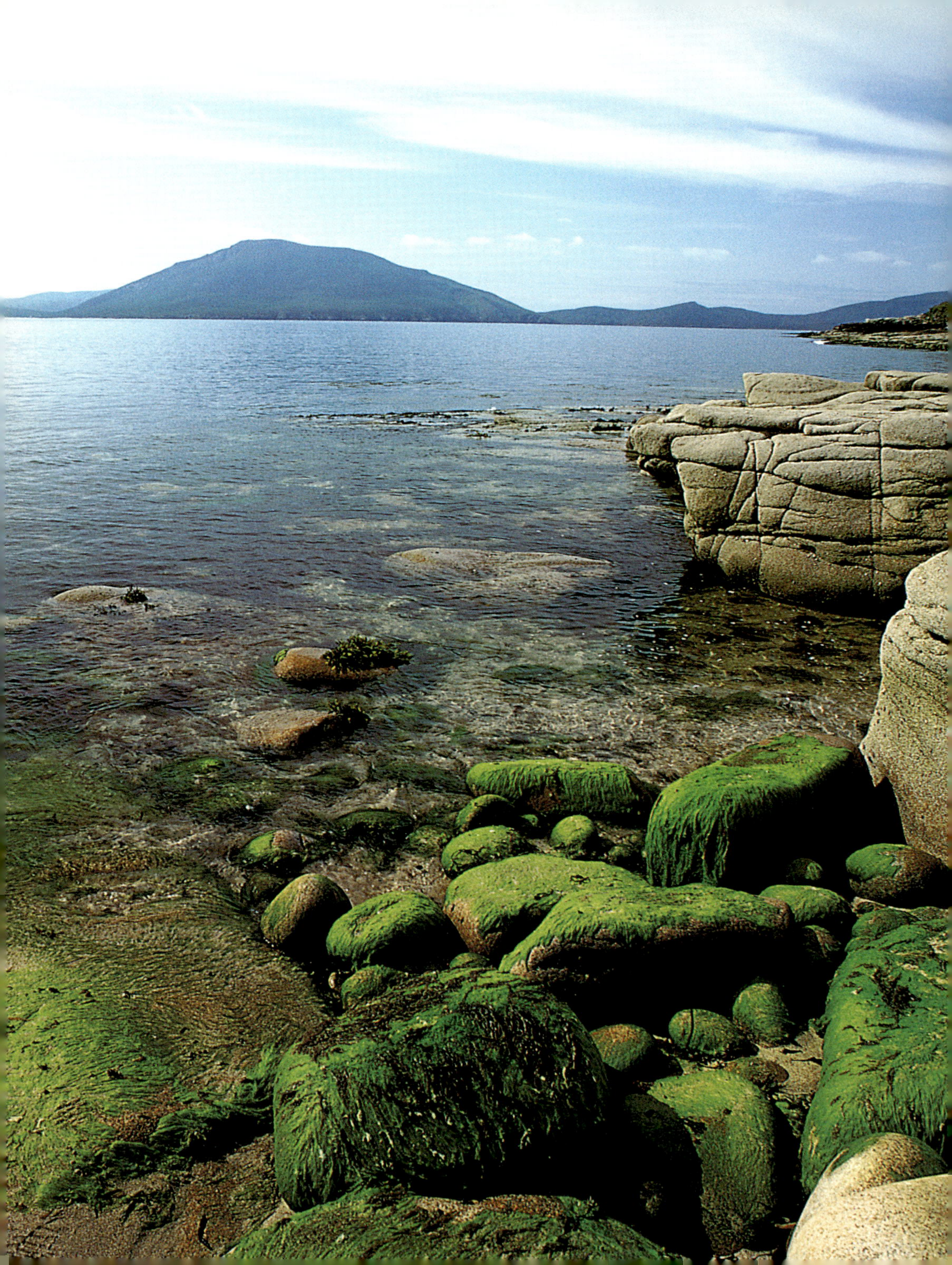

*N*ow with the coming in of the
spring the days will stretch a bit,
And after the Feast of Brigid I shall
hoist my flag and go,
For since the thought got into my
head I can neither stand nor sit
Until I find myself in the middle of
the County of Mayo.
  —Translated from the Gaelic by
  James Stephens (1882–1950)

BLACKSOD BAY, COUNTY MAYO

s	m	t	w	t	f	s
		1	2	3	4	5
6	7	8	9	10	11	12
13	14	15	16	17	18	19
20	21	22	23	24	25	26
27	28	29	30	31		

MAY

VICTORIA DAY (CANADA)

monday
21 141

tuesday
22 142

wednesday
☽ **23** 143

thursday
24 144

friday
25 145

saturday
26 146

sunday
27 147

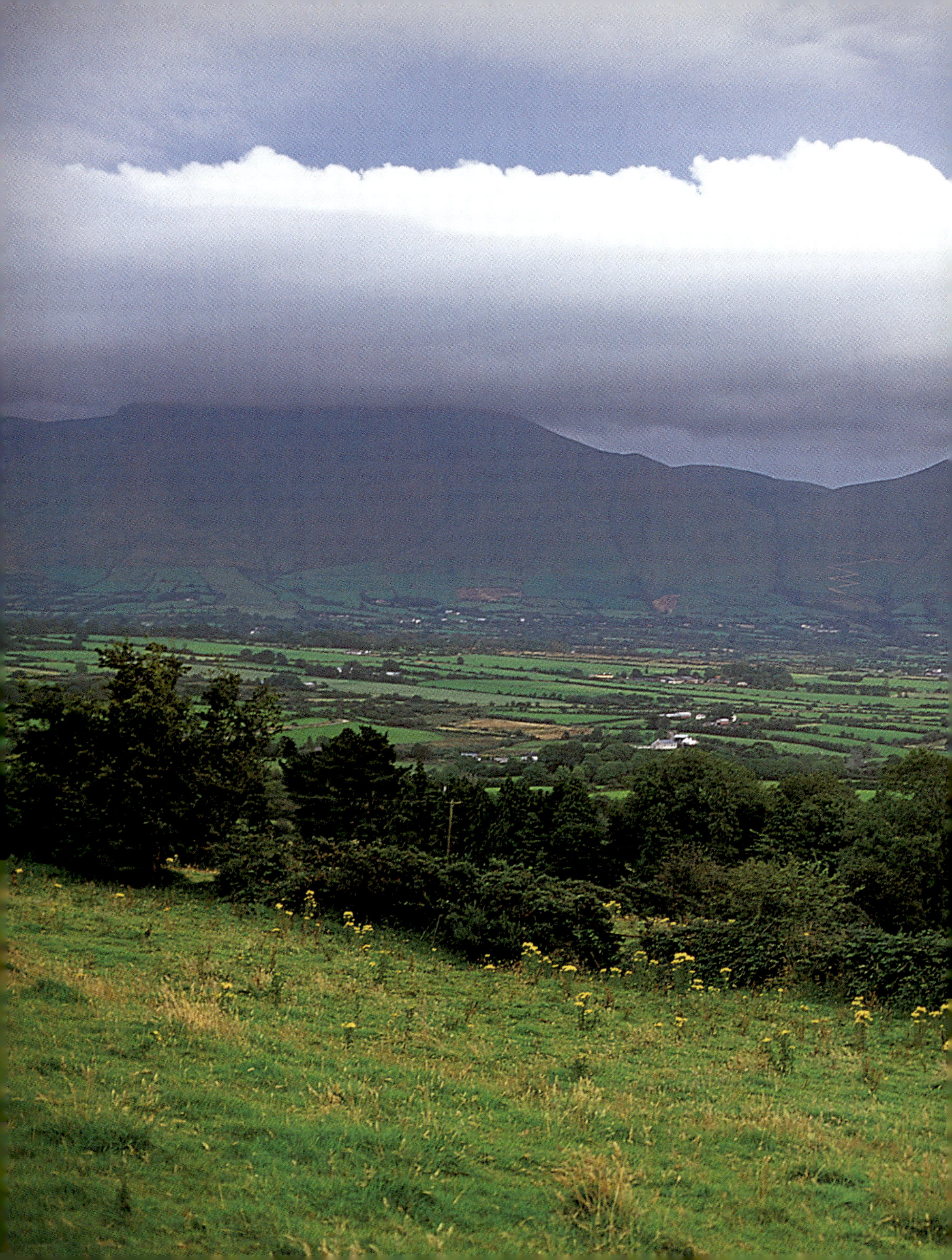

*I always pass on good advice.
It is the only thing to do with
it. It is never of any use to oneself.*
—Oscar Wilde (1854–1900)

MEMORIAL DAY OBSERVED
BANK HOLIDAY (UK)

monday

28 148

tuesday

29 149

MEMORIAL DAY

wednesday

30 150

thursday

31 151

friday

○ 1 152

GLEN OF AHERLOW,
COUNTY TIPPERARY

saturday

2 153

sunday

3 154

s	m	t	w	t	f	s
					1	2
3	4	5	6	7	8	9
10	11	12	13	14	15	16
17	18	19	20	21	22	23
24	25	26	27	28	29	30

JUNE

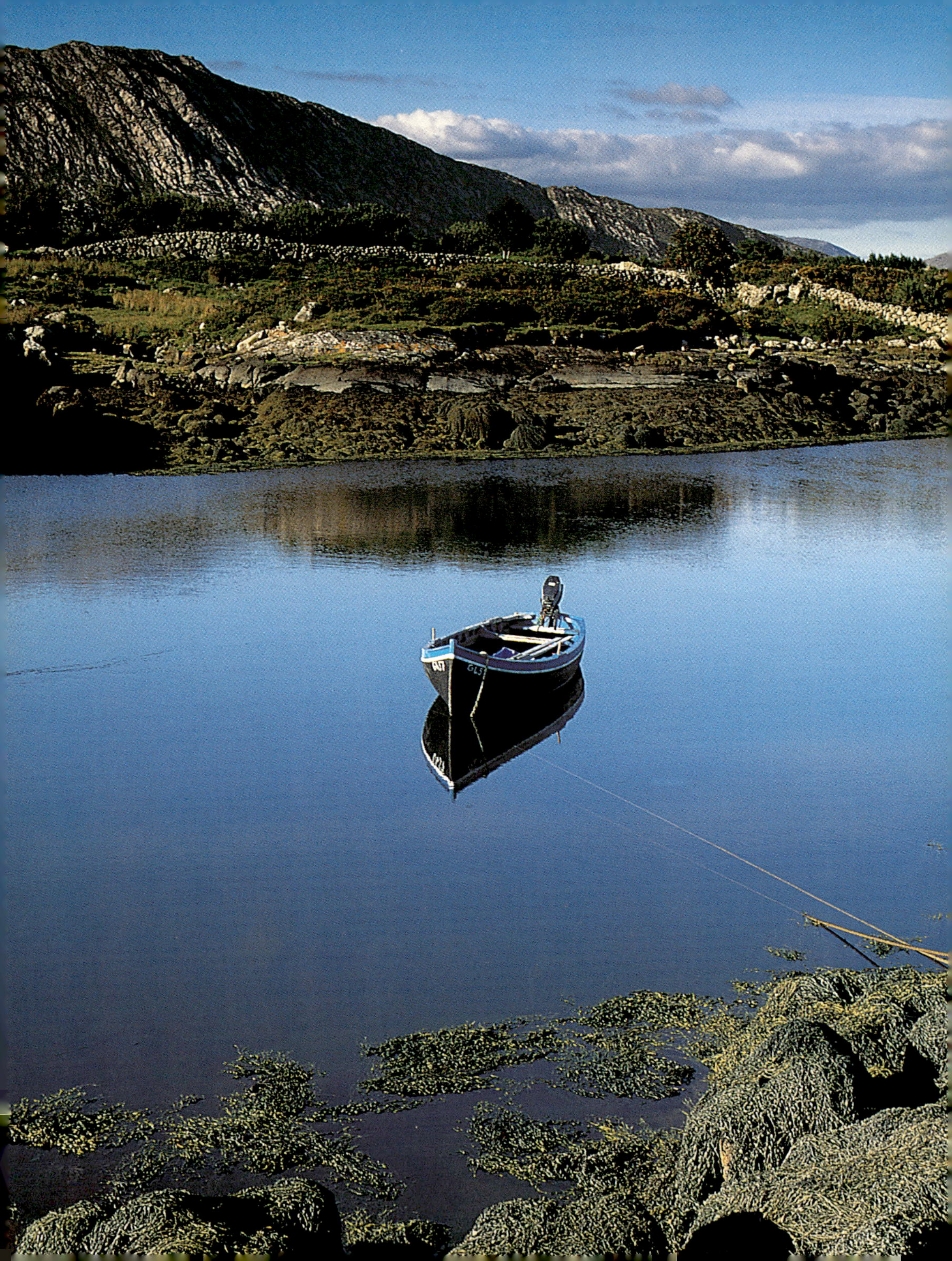

The only business of the head in the world is to bow a ceaseless obeisance to the heart.
—William Butler Yeats (1865–1939)

monday

4   155

tuesday

5   156

wednesday

6   157

thursday

7   158

friday

☾ 8   159

KILKIERAN BAY, COUNTY GALWAY

saturday

9   160

s	m	t	w	t	f	s
					1	2
3	4	5	6	7	8	9
10	11	12	13	14	15	16
17	18	19	20	21	22	23
24	25	26	27	28	29	30

JUNE

sunday

10   161

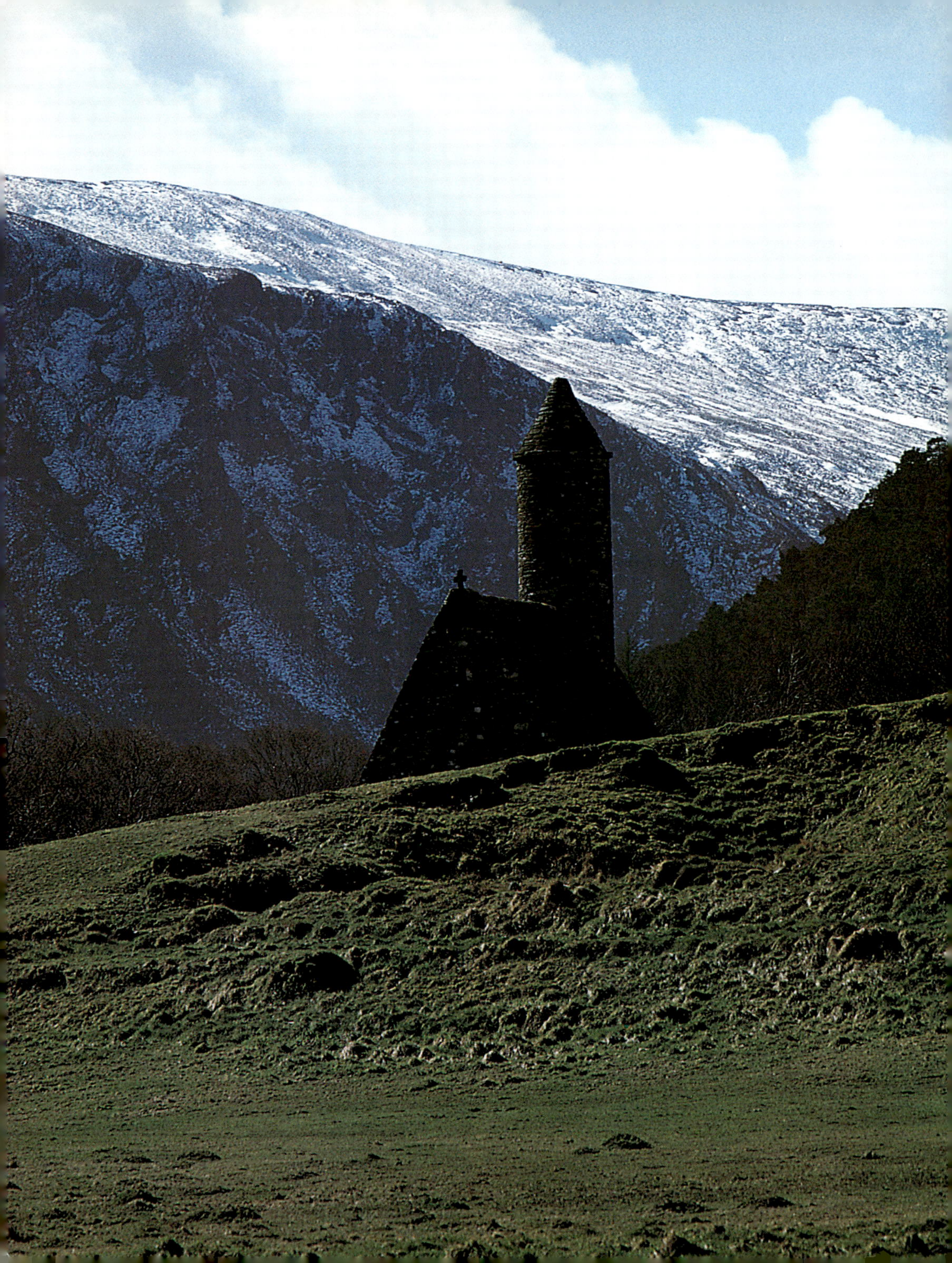

I was born on a storm-swept rock and hate the soft growth of sun-baked lands where there is no frost in men's bones.
—Liam O'Flaherty (1896–1984)

GLENDALOUGH, COUNTY WICKLOW

s	m	t	w	t	f	s
					1	2
3	4	5	6	7	8	9
10	11	12	13	14	15	16
17	18	19	20	21	22	23
24	25	26	27	28	29	30

JUNE

monday
11 162

tuesday
12 163

wednesday
13 164

FLAG DAY *thursday*
14 165

friday
● **15** 166

saturday
16 167

FATHER'S DAY *sunday*
17 168

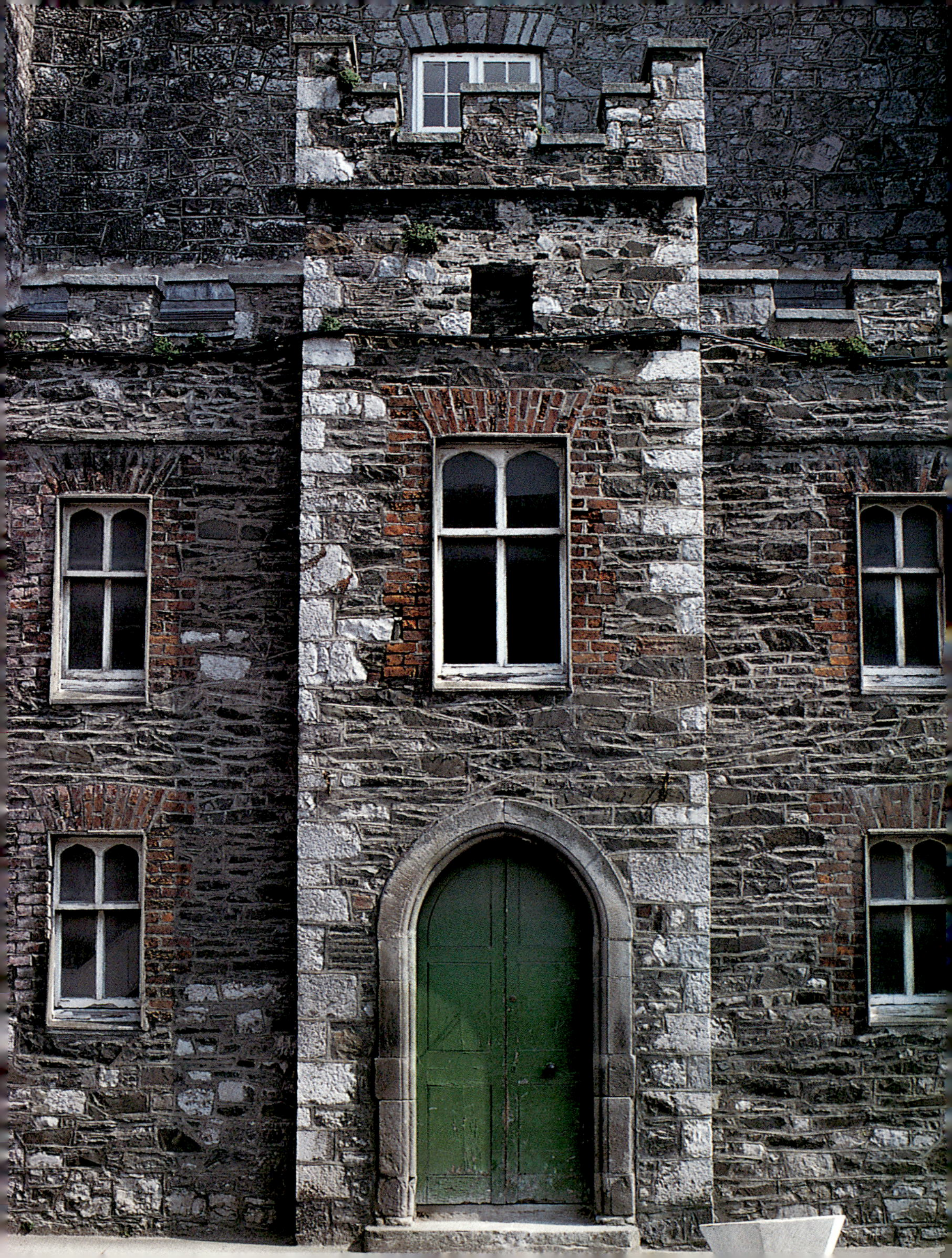

*In a good play every speech should
be as fully flavoured as a nut or
apple.*
—J. M. Synge·(1871–1909)

monday

18 169

tuesday

19 170

wednesday

20 171

SUMMER SOLSTICE 6:06 PM (GMT)   *thursday*

21 172

friday

☽ **22** 173

ARDEE, COUNTY LOUTH

saturday

23 174

s	m	t	w	t	f	s
					1	2
3	4	5	6	7	8	9
10	11	12	13	14	15	16
17	18	19	20	21	22	23
24	25	26	27	28	29	30

JUNE

sunday

24 175

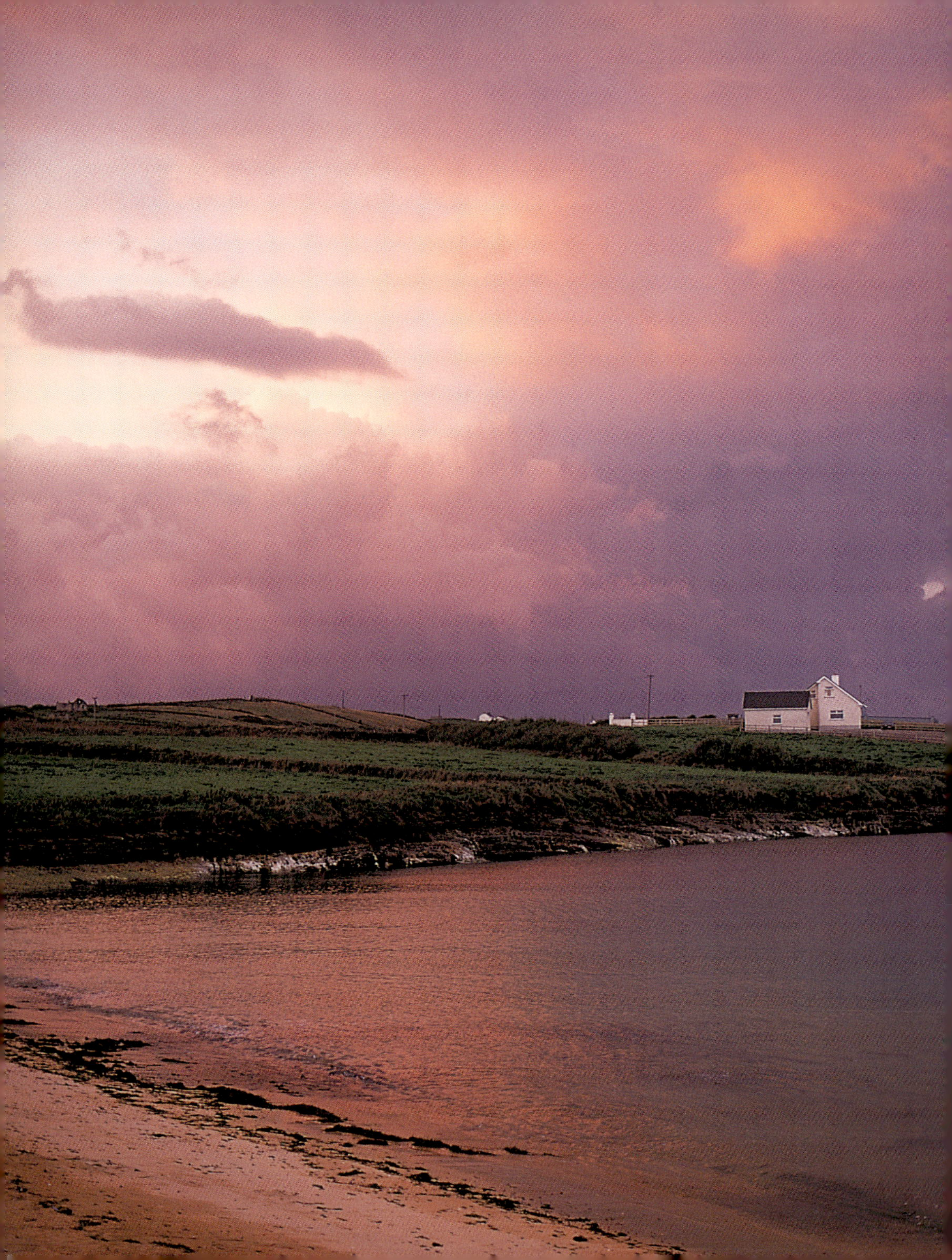

The safest road to hell is the gradual one—the gentle slope, soft underfoot, without sudden turnings, without milestones, without signposts.
                —C. S. Lewis (1898–1963)

monday

25 176

tuesday

26 177

wednesday

27 178

thursday

28 179

friday

29 180

RABLEY HILL, COUNTY DONEGAL

saturday

○ **30** 181

s	m	t	w	t	f	s
1	2	3	4	5	6	7
8	9	10	11	12	13	14
15	16	17	18	19	20	21
22	23	24	25	26	27	28
29	30	31				

JULY

CANADA DAY (CANADA)

sunday

1 182

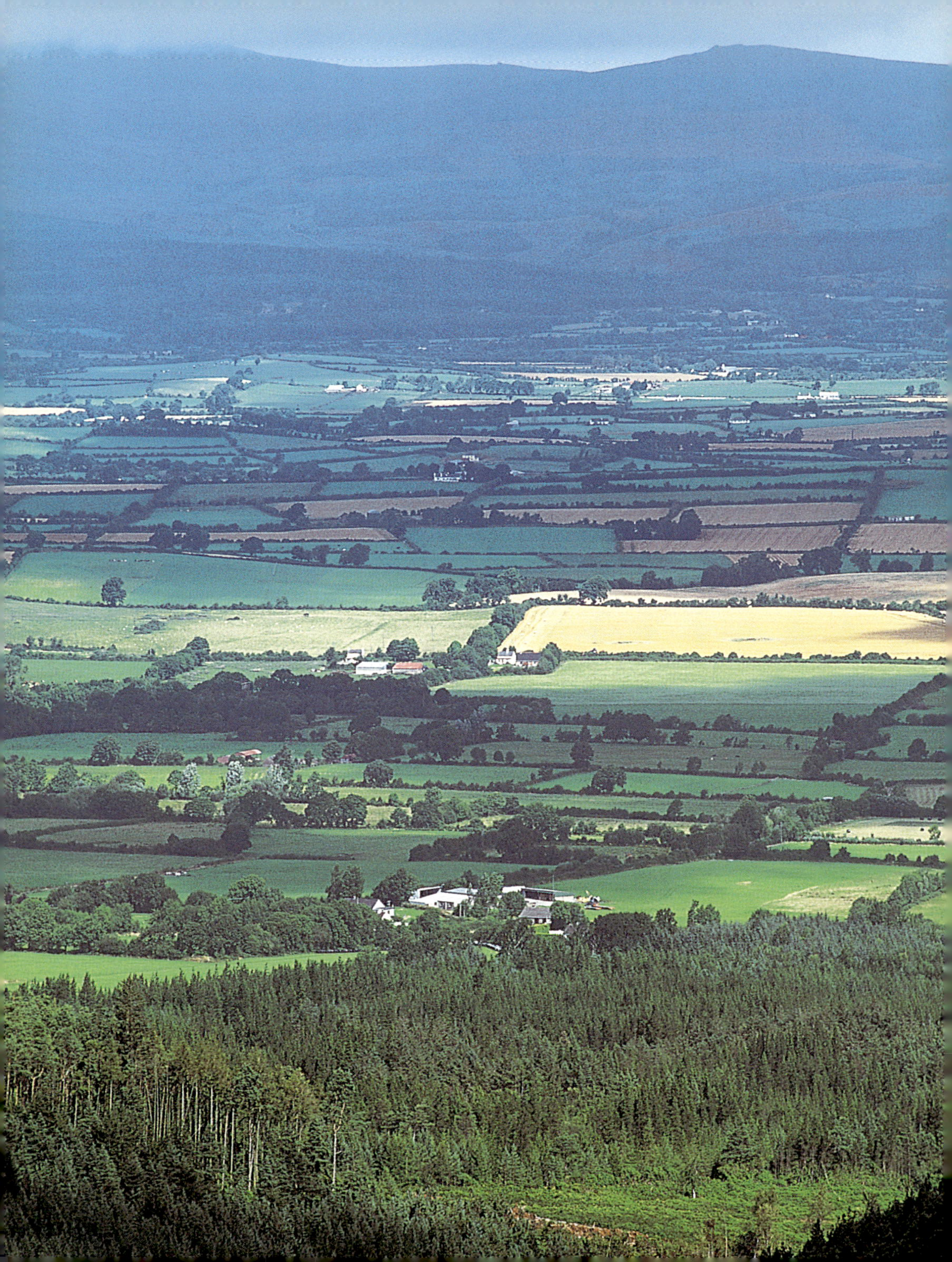

JULY

Wisdom is the comb given to a man after he has lost his hair.
—J. P. Dunleavy (b. 1926)

CANADA DAY OBSERVED (CANADA)

monday

2 183

tuesday

3 184

INDEPENDENCE DAY

wednesday

4 185

thursday

5 186

friday

6 187

KNOCKMEALDOWN MOUNTAINS,
COUNTY TIPPERARY

saturday

☾ 7 188

sunday

8 189

s	m	t	w	t	f	s
1	2	3	4	5	6	7
8	9	10	11	12	13	14
15	16	17	18	19	20	21
22	23	24	25	26	27	28
29	30	31				

JULY

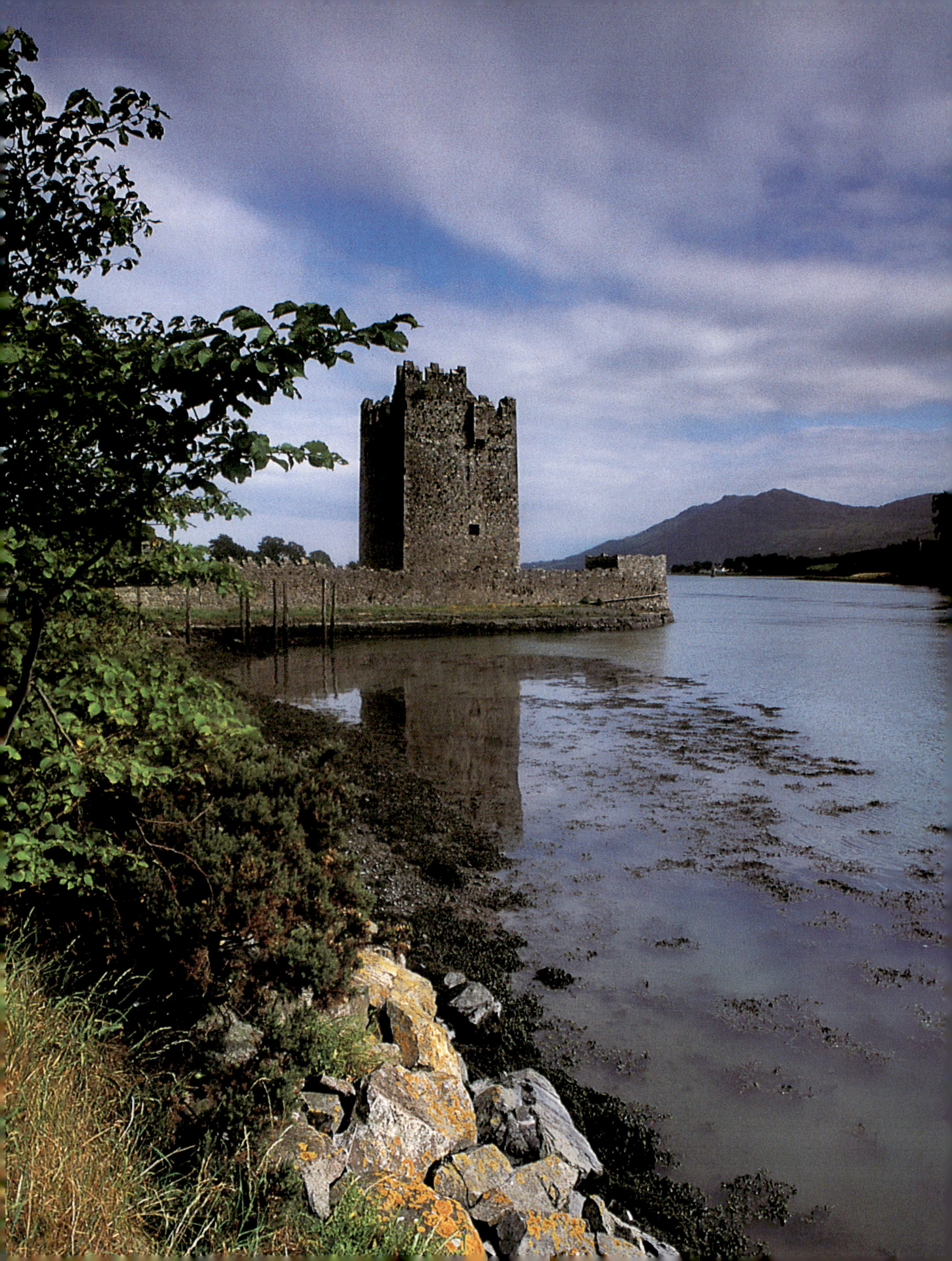

JULY

*O*ft, in the stilly night,
 Ere slumber's chain has bound me,
Fond Memory brings the light
Of other days around me:
The smiles, the tears
Of boyhood's years,
The words of love then spoken;
The eyes that shone,
Now dimm'd and gone,
The cheerful hearts now broken!
Thus, in the stilly night,
Ere slumber's chain has bound me,
Sad Memory brings the light
Of other days around me.
          —Thomas Moore (1779–1852)

monday

9 190

tuesday

10 191

wednesday

11 192

BANK HOLIDAY (N. IRELAND)   *thursday*

12 193

friday

13 194

NARROW WATER CASTLE,
COUNTY DOWN

saturday

● **14** 195

s	m	t	w	t	f	s
1	2	3	4	5	6	7
8	9	10	11	12	13	14
15	16	17	18	19	20	21
22	23	24	25	26	27	28
29	30	31				

JULY

sunday

15 196

'Tis a strange thing ... that among us people can't agree the whole week, because they go different ways upon Sundays.
—George Farquhar (1678–1707)

monday

16 197

tuesday

17 198

wednesday

18 199

thursday

19 200

friday

20 201

KILCOOLAGHT EAST OGHAM STONE,
REASK, COUNTY KERRY

saturday

21 202

s	m	t	w	t	f	s
1	2	3	4	5	6	7
8	9	10	11	12	13	14
15	16	17	18	19	20	21
22	23	24	25	26	27	28
29	30	31				

sunday

☽ **22** 203

JULY

I stood beside a pool, from whence
   ascended,
Mounting the cloudy platforms of
      the wind,
A stately heron; its soaring I attended,
Till it grew dim, and I with watching
      blind—
When lo! a shaft of arrowy light
      descended
Upon its darkness and its dim attire;
It straightway kindled them, and was
      afire,
And with the unconsuming radiance
      blended.
And bird, a cloud, flecking the sunny
      air,
It had its golden dwelling 'mid the
      lightning
Of those empyreal domes, and it
      might there
Have dwelt for ever, glorified and
      bright'ning,
But that its wings were weak—so it
      became
A dusky speck again, that was a
      winged flame.
                    —Richard Chenevix Trench
                         (1807–1886)

DOON LOUGH, COUNTY LEITRIM

monday

23 204

tuesday

24 205

wednesday

25 206

thursday

26 207

friday

27 208

saturday

28 209

sunday

29 210

s	m	t	w	t	f	s
1	2	3	4	5	6	7
8	9	10	11	12	13	14
15	16	17	18	19	20	21
22	23	24	25	26	27	28
29	30	31				

JULY

*S*ilent, o Moyle, be the roar of thy water,
Break not, ye breezes, your chain of repose,
While, murmuring mournfully, Lir's lonely daughter
Tells to the night-star her tale of woes.
    —Thomas Moore (1779-1852)

WICKLOW GAP, COUNTY WICKLOW

s	m	t	w	t	f	s
			1	2	3	4
5	6	7	8	9	10	11
12	13	14	15	16	17	18
19	20	21	22	23	24	25
26	27	28	29	30	31	

AUGUST

monday
30 211

tuesday
31 212

wednesday
1 213

thursday
2 214

friday
3 215

saturday
4 216

sunday
5 217

Our Irish blunders are never blunders of the heart.
—Maria Edgeworth (1767–1849)

monday

6 218

tuesday

7 219

wednesday

8 220

thursday

9 221

friday

10 222

**BALLYNACARRIGA CASTLE,
COUNTY CORK**

saturday

11 223

s	m	t	w	t	f	s
			1	2	3	4
5	6	7	8	9	10	11
12	13	14	15	16	17	18
19	20	21	22	23	24	25
26	27	28	29	30	31	

AUGUST

sunday

⬤ **12** 224

AUGUST

An Irish novelist gets from the Irish people a certain reverence, a good measure of kindliness, considerable latitude in conduct and thought: in fine he gets his due from a God-fearing people. But he must not forget that his first duty is homeward.

—Donn Byrne (1889–1929)

CHURCH OF ST. JOHN THE BAPTIST,
KILMACDUAGH, COUNTY GALWAY

s	m	t	w	t	f	s
			1	2	3	4
5	6	7	8	9	10	11
12	13	14	15	16	17	18
19	20	21	22	23	24	25
26	27	28	29	30	31	

AUGUST

monday
13 225

tuesday
14 226

wednesday
15 227

thursday
16 228

friday
17 229

saturday
18 230

sunday
19 231

May you live all the days of your life.
—Jonathan Swift (1667–1745)

monday
☽ **20** 232

tuesday
21 233

wednesday
22 234

thursday
23 235

friday
24 236

FLOWERY WELLINGTON BOOTS

saturday
25 237

sunday
26 238

s	m	t	w	t	f	s
			1	2	3	4
5	6	7	8	9	10	11
12	13	14	15	16	17	18
19	20	21	22	23	24	25
26	27	28	29	30	31	

AUGUST

*S*atire is a sort of glass, wherein beholders do generally discover everybody's face but their own; which is the chief reason for that kind of reception it meets in the world, and that so very few are offended with it.

—Jonathan Swift (1667–1745)

BANK HOLIDAY (UK EXCEPT SCOTLAND)

monday

27 239

tuesday

28 240

wednesday

29 241

thursday

30 242

friday

31 243

PARKE'S CASTLE, COUNTY LEITRIM

saturday

1 244

sunday

2 245

s	m	t	w	t	f	s
						1
2	3	4	5	6	7	8
9	10	11	12	13	14	15
16	17	18	19	20	21	22
23	24	25	26	27	28	29
30			SEPTEMBER			

SEPTEMBER

I found in Munster, unfettered of any,
Kings and queens, and poets a many—
Poets well skilled in music and measure,
Prosperous doings, mirth and pleasure.
—James Clarence Mangan
(1803–1849)

monday

3   246

tuesday

☾ 4   247

wednesday

5   248

thursday

6   249

friday

7   250

KILMALLOCK,
COUNTY LIMERICK

saturday

8   251

sunday

9   252

s	m	t	w	t	f	s
						1
2	3	4	5	6	7	8
9	10	11	12	13	14	15
16	17	18	19	20	21	22
23	24	25	26	27	28	29
30			SEPTEMBER			

SEPTEMBER

*We make out of the quarrel
with others, rhetoric, but of
the quarrel with ourselves, poetry.*
—William Butler Yeats (1865–1939)

monday

10 253

tuesday

⬤ **11** 254

ROSH HASHANAH (BEGINS AT SUNSET)   *wednesday*

12 255

thursday

13 256

friday

14 257

GLENCOLUMBKILLE,
COUNTY DONEGAL

saturday

15 258

s	m	t	w	t	f	s
						1
2	3	4	5	6	7	8
9	10	11	12	13	14	15
16	17	18	19	20	21	22
23	24	25	26	27	28	29
30			SEPTEMBER			

sunday

16 259

A hedge before me, one behind,
a blackbird sings from that,
above my small book many-lined
I apprehend his chat.
Up trees, in costumes buff,
mild accurate cuckoos bleat.
Lord love me, good the stuff
I write in a shady seat.
    —Translated from the Gaelic by
        Flann O'Brien (1911–1966)

monday

17 260

tuesday

18 261

wednesday

☽ **19** 262

thursday

20 263

YOM KIPPUR (BEGINS AT SUNSET)

friday

21 264

KILMALLOCK CHURCH,
COUNTY LIMERICK

saturday

22 265

s	m	t	w	t	f	s
						1
2	3	4	5	6	7	8
9	10	11	12	13	14	15
16	17	18	19	20	21	22
23	24	25	26	27	28	29
30			SEPTEMBER			

AUTUMNAL EQUINOX 9:51 AM (GMT)

sunday

23 266

*M*y one claim to originality
among Irishmen is that I have
never made a speech.
—George Moore (1852–1933)

monday

24 267

tuesday

25 268

wednesday

○ 26 269

thursday

27 270

friday

28 271

BRANDON BAY, COUNTY KERRY

saturday

29 272

s	m	t	w	t	f	s
						1
2	3	4	5	6	7	8
9	10	11	12	13	14	15
16	17	18	19	20	21	22
23	24	25	26	27	28	29
30			SEPTEMBER			

sunday

30 273

I don't know how it is, but throughout the country the men and the landscapes seem to be the same, and one and the other seem ragged, ruined, and cheerful.
—William Makepeace Thackeray
(1811–1863)

HORN HEAD, COUNTY DONEGAL

s	m	t	w	t	f	s
	1	2	3	4	5	6
7	8	9	10	11	12	13
14	15	16	17	18	19	20
21	22	23	24	25	26	27
28	29	30	31			

OCTOBER

monday

1 274

tuesday

2 275

wednesday

☾ 3 276

thursday

4 277

friday

5 278

saturday

6 279

sunday

7 280

I have a hut here in the wood
that nobody knows but my Lord.
An ash tree one side is its wall,
the other a hazel, a great rath tree.
— The hermit Marbáin to
King Guaire (ninth century)

monday

8 281

tuesday

9 282

wednesday

10 283

thursday

11 284

COLUMBUS DAY

friday

12 285

COTTAGES, COUNTY KERRY

saturday

13 286

sunday

14 287

s	m	t	w	t	f	s
	1	2	3	4	5	6
7	8	9	10	11	12	13
14	15	16	17	18	19	20
21	22	23	24	25	26	27
28	29	30	31			

OCTOBER

OCTOBER

A tune is more lasting than the
voice of the birds,
A word is more lasting than the
riches of the world....
—Douglas Hyde (1860–1949)

monday

15 <small>288</small>

tuesday

16 <small>289</small>

wednesday

17 <small>290</small>

thursday

18 <small>291</small>

friday

☽ 19 <small>292</small>

SLIGO-LEITRIM BORDER

saturday

20 <small>293</small>

s	m	t	w	t	f	s
	1	2	3	4	5	6
7	8	9	10	11	12	13
14	15	16	17	18	19	20
21	22	23	24	25	26	27
28	29	30	31			

OCTOBER

sunday

21 <small>294</small>

*I*t is impossible to read the daily press without being diverted from reality. You are full of enthusiasm for the eternal verities—life is worth living, and then out of sinful curiosity you open a newspaper. You are disillusioned and wrecked.
—Patrick Kavanaugh (1905–1967)

monday

22 295

tuesday

23 296

UNITED NATIONS DAY **wednesday**

24 297

thursday

25 298

friday

○ **26** 299

COTTAGE, COUNTY WATERFORD

saturday

27 300

s	m	t	w	t	f	s
	1	2	3	4	5	6
7	8	9	10	11	12	13
14	15	16	17	18	19	20
21	22	23	24	25	26	27
28	29	30	31			

OCTOBER

SUMMER TIME ENDS (UK) **sunday**

28 301

Get the advice of everybody whose opinion is worth having—they are very few—and then do what you think best yourself.
—Charles Stewart Parnell
(1846–1891)

monday

29 302

tuesday

30 303

HALLOWEEN *wednesday*

31 304

thursday

☾ 1 305

friday

2 306

TIMOLEAGUE FRANCISCAN FRIARY,
COUNTY CORK

saturday

3 307

s	m	t	w	t	f	s
				1	2	3
4	5	6	7	8	9	10
11	12	13	14	15	16	17
18	19	20	21	22	23	24
25	26	27	28	29	30	

NOVEMBER

DAYLIGHT SAVING TIME ENDS *sunday*

4 308

NOVEMBER

Whenever the clergy succeeded in conquering political power in any country, the result has been disastrous to the interests of religion and inimical to the progress of humanity.
—James Connolly (1868–1916)

STRADE FRIARY,
COUNTY MAYO

s	m	t	w	t	f	s
				1	2	3
4	5	6	7	8	9	10
11	12	13	14	15	16	17
18	19	20	21	22	23	24
25	26	27	28	29	30	

NOVEMBER

monday
5 309

tuesday
6 310

wednesday
7 311

thursday
8 312

friday
9 313

saturday
10 314

VETERANS DAY
REMEMBRANCE DAY (CANADA)

sunday
11 315

*I*rishness is not primarily a question of birth or blood or language; it is the condition of being involved in the Irish situation, and usually of being mauled by it.

—Conor Cruise O'Brien (b. 1917)

monday

12 316

tuesday

13 317

wednesday

14 318

thursday

15 319

friday

16 320

BEEBANE POINT, DINGLE,
COUNTY KERRY

saturday

☽ **17** 321

sunday

18 322

s	m	t	w	t	f	s
				1	2	3
4	5	6	7	8	9	10
11	12	13	14	15	16	17
18	19	20	21	22	23	24
25	26	27	28	29	30	

NOVEMBER

NOVEMBER

*A*t the court of King Laoghaire,
Patrick explained that there is
only one God but that He is tripar-
tite: Father, Son, and Holy Ghost. To
illustrate this mystery, Patrick bent
and plucked a shamrock sprig:
"Here is one stem but three leaves.
In God, the Trinity arises from the
one divinity."
— Peter Somerville-Large (b. 1928)

monday

19 323

tuesday

20 324

wednesday

21 325

THANKSGIVING DAY

thursday

22 326

friday

23 327

BALLYBOGGAN ABBEY, WEST MEATH

saturday

○ **24** 328

s	m	t	w	t	f	s
				1	2	3
4	5	6	7	8	9	10
11	12	13	14	15	16	17
18	19	20	21	22	23	24
25	26	27	28	29	30	

NOVEMBER

sunday

25 329

*So simple is the earth we tread,
So quick with love and life her
    frame,
Ten thousand years have dawned
    and fled,
And still her magic is the same.*
    —Stopford A. Brooke (1832–1916)

monday

26 330

tuesday

27 331

wednesday

28 332

thursday

29 333

friday

30 334

COURTMACSHERRY BAY,
COUNTY CORK

saturday

☾ **1** 335

s	m	t	w	t	f	s
						1
2	3	4	5	6	7	8
9	10	11	12	13	14	15
16	17	18	19	20	21	22
23	24	25	26	27	28	29
30	31		DECEMBER			

sunday

2 336

DECEMBER

*W*hen anyone asks me about
the Irish character, I say look
at the trees. Maimed, stark and mis-
shapen, but ferociously tenacious.
—Edna O'Brien (b. 1932)

monday

3 337

HANUKKAH (BEGINS AT SUNSET) *tuesday*

4 338

wednesday

5 339

thursday

6 340

friday

7 341

TREE IN FIELD, COUNTY MEATH

saturday

8 342

s	m	t	w	t	f	s
						1
2	3	4	5	6	7	8
9	10	11	12	13	14	15
16	17	18	19	20	21	22
23	24	25	26	27	28	29
30	31				DECEMBER	

sunday

9 343

DECEMBER

We . . . are no petty people. We are one of the great stocks of Burke; we are the people of Swift, the people of Emmet, the people of Parnell.
—William Butler Yeats (1865–1939)

monday

10 344

tuesday

11 345

wednesday

12 346

thursday

13 347

friday

14 348

KYLEMORE ABBEY, COUNTY GALWAY

saturday

15 349

s	m	t	w	t	f	s
						1
2	3	4	5	6	7	8
9	10	11	12	13	14	15
16	17	18	19	20	21	22
23	24	25	26	27	28	29
30	31					

DECEMBER

sunday

16 350

DECEMBER

*W*riting in English is the most
ingenious torture ever devised
for sins committed in previous lives.
—James Joyce (1882–1941)

monday

☽ **17** 351

tuesday

18 352

wednesday

19 353

thursday

20 354

friday

21 355

CASTLETOWNSHEND,
SOUTHWEST CORK

WINTER SOLSTICE 6:08 AM (GMT)   *saturday*

22 356

s	m	t	w	t	f	s
						1
2	3	4	5	6	7	8
9	10	11	12	13	14	15
16	17	18	19	20	21	22
23	24	25	26	27	28	29
30	31		DECEMBER			

sunday

23 357

DECEMBER

Still south I went and west and south again,
Through Wicklow from the morning till the night,
And far from cities, and the sights of men,
Lived with the sunshine, and the moon's delight.
   —AE (George Russell) (1867–1935)

monday

○ **24** 358

CHRISTMAS DAY

tuesday

25 359

BOXING DAY (CANADA, UK)

KWANZAA BEGINS

wednesday

26 360

thursday

27 361

friday

28 362

GLENDALOUGH, COUNTY WICKLOW

saturday

29 363

s	m	t	w	t	f	s
						1
2	3	4	5	6	7	8
9	10	11	12	13	14	15
16	17	18	19	20	21	22
23	24	25	26	27	28	29
30	31				DECEMBER	

sunday

30 364

*C*hill the winter, cold the wind,
  Up the stag springs, stark of
    mind;
Fierce and bare the mountain fells—
But the brave stag boldly bells.
    —Translated from the Gaelic by
      George Sigerson (1836–1925)

	monday
	☾ **31** 365

NEW YEAR'S DAY	tuesday
	1 1

BANK HOLIDAY (SCOTLAND)	wednesday
	2 2

	thursday
	3 3

	friday
	4 4

	saturday
	5 5

KILCARN BRIDGE, COUNTY MEATH

s	m	t	w	t	f	s
		1	2	3	4	5
6	7	8	9	10	11	12
13	14	15	16	17	18	19
20	21	22	23	24	25	26
27	28	29	30	31		

JANUARY

	sunday
	6 6

2007 INTERNATIONAL HOLIDAYS

Following are the observed dates of major (bank-closing) holidays for selected countries in 2007. Islamic observances are subject to adjustment. Holidays for the US, UK, and Canada and major Jewish holidays appear on this calendar's grid pages. Pomegranate is not responsible for errors or omissions in this list. Users of this information should confirm dates with local sources before making international travel or business plans.

ARGENTINA

1 Jan	New Year's Day
2 Apr	Malvinas Islands Memorial
5 Apr	Holy Thursday
6 Apr	Good Friday
8 Apr	Easter
1 May	Labor Day
25 May	Revolution Day
18 Jun	Flag Day
9 Jul	Independence Day
20 Aug	General San Martin Anniversary
15 Oct	Día de la Raza
8 Dec	Immaculate Conception
25 Dec	Christmas

AUSTRALIA

1 Jan	New Year's Day
26 Jan	Australia Day
5 Mar	Labor Day (WA)
12 Mar	Labor Day (Vic) Eight Hours Day (Tas)
19 Mar	Canberra Day (ACT)
6 Apr	Good Friday
7–9 Apr	Easter Holiday
25 Apr	Anzac Day
7 May	Labor Day (Qld) May Day (NT)
4 Jun	Foundation Day (WA)
11 Jun	Queen's Birthday
6 Aug	Bank Holiday (NSW, NT)
1 Oct	Labor Day (NSW, ACT, SA)
25 Dec	Christmas
26 Dec	Boxing Day

BRAZIL

1 Jan	New Year's Day
20 Jan	São Sebastião Day (Rio de Janeiro)
25 Jan	São Paulo Anniversary (São Paulo)
19–20 Feb	Carnival
6 Apr	Good Friday
8 Apr	Easter
21 Apr	Tiradentes Day
1 May	Labor Day
7 Jun	Corpus Christi
9 Jul	State Holiday (São Paulo)
7 Sep	Independence Day
12 Oct	Our Lady of Aparecida
2 Nov	All Souls' Day
15 Nov	Proclamation of the Republic
20 Nov	Zumbi dos Palmares Day (Rio de Janeiro)
25 Dec	Christmas

CHINA (SEE ALSO HONG KONG)

1 Jan	New Year's Day
18–20 Feb	Lunar New Year
8 Mar	Women's Day
1–3 May	Labor Day Holiday
4 May	Youth Day
1 June	Children's Day
1 Aug	Army Day
1–3 Oct	National Holiday

FRANCE

1 Jan	New Year's Day
8–9 Apr	Easter Holiday
1 May	Labor Day
8 May	Armistice Day (WWII)
17 May	Ascension Day
27–28 May	Pentecost/Whitmonday
14 Jul	Bastille Day
15 Aug	Assumption Day
1 Nov	All Saints' Day
11 Nov	Armistice Day (WWI)
25 Dec	Christmas

GERMANY

1 Jan	New Year's Day
6 Jan	Epiphany*
6 Apr	Good Friday
8–9 Apr	Easter Holiday
1 May	Labor Day
17 May	Ascension Day
27–28 May	Pentecost/Whitmonday
7 Jun	Corpus Christi*
15 Aug	Assumption Day*
3 Oct	Unity Day
31 Oct	Reformation Day*
1 Nov	All Saints' Day*
21 Nov	Penance Day*
24–26 Dec	Christmas Holiday
31 Dec	New Year's Eve

*Observed only in some states

HONG KONG

1 Jan	New Year's Day
17–20 Feb	Lunar New Year
5 Apr	Ching Ming Festival
6–9 Apr	Easter Holiday
1 May	Labor Day
24 May	Buddha's Birthday
19 Jun	Tuen Ng Day
2 Jul	SAR Establishment Day
26 Sep	Mid-Autumn Festival
1 Oct	Chinese National Holiday
19 Oct	Chung Yeung Festival
25–26 Dec	Christmas Holiday

INDIA

20 Jan	Muharram (Islamic New Year)
26 Jan	Republic Day
31 Mar	Prophet Muhammad's Birthday Mahavir Jayanthi
6 Apr	Good Friday
2 May	Buddha Purnima
15 Aug	Independence Day
2 Oct	Mahatma Gandhi's Birthday
13 Oct	Ramzan Id (Eid-al-Fitr)
21 Oct	Dussehra
9 Nov	Diwali (Deepavali)
24 Nov	Guru Nanak's Birthday
20 Dec	Bakr-Id (Eid-al-Adha)
25 Dec	Christmas

Additional holidays to be declared

IRELAND

1 Jan	New Year's Day
17 Mar	St. Patrick's Day
8–9 Apr	Easter Holiday
7 May	May Holiday
4 Jun	June Holiday
6 Aug	August Holiday
29 Oct	October Holiday
25 Dec	Christmas
26 Dec	St. Stephen's Day

ISRAEL

4 Mar	Purim
3 Apr	First day of Pesach
9 Apr	Last day of Pesach
22 Apr	Memorial Day
23 Apr	Independence Day
23 May	Shavuot
24 Jul	Fast of Av
13–14 Sep	Rosh Hashanah
21–22 Sep	Yom Kippur
27 Sep	First day of Sukkot
4–5 Oct	Shemini Atzeret/Simhat Torah

ITALY

1 Jan	New Year's Day
6 Jan	Epiphany
8–9 Apr	Easter Holiday
25 Apr	Liberation Day
1 May	Labor Day
2 Jun	Republic Day
29 Jun	Sts. Peter and Paul (Rome)
15 Aug	Assumption Day
1 Nov	All Saints' Day
8 Dec	Immaculate Conception
25 Dec	Christmas
26 Dec	St. Stephen's Day

2007 INTERNATIONAL HOLIDAYS

Japan
1 Jan	New Year's Day
8 Jan	Coming of Age Day
12 Feb	National Foundation Day
21 Mar	Vernal Equinox Holiday
30 Apr	Greenery Day
3 May	Constitution Day
4 May	National Holiday
5 May	Children's Day
16 Jul	Marine Day
17 Sep	Respect for the Aged Day
24 Sep	Autumnal Equinox Holiday
8 Oct	Health and Sports Day
3 Nov	Culture Day
23 Nov	Labor Thanksgiving Day
24 Dec	Emperor's Birthday

Kenya
1 Jan	New Year's Day
6 Apr	Good Friday
8–9 Apr	Easter Holiday
1 May	Labor Day
1 Jun	Madaraka Day
10 Oct	Moi Day
13 Oct	Eid-al-Fitr
20 Oct	Kenyatta Day
12 Dec	Jamhuri Day
25 Dec	Christmas
26 Dec	Boxing Day

Mexico
1 Jan	New Year's Day
5 Feb	Constitution Day
21 Mar	Benito Juárez's Birthday
5 Apr	Holy Thursday
6 Apr	Good Friday
8 Apr	Easter
1 May	Labor Day
5 May	Battle of Puebla
16 Sep	Independence Day
1 Nov	All Saints' Day
2 Nov	Day of the Dead
20 Nov	Revolution Day
12 Dec	Our Lady of Guadalupe
25 Dec	Christmas

Netherlands
1 Jan	New Year's Day
6 Apr	Good Friday
8–9 Apr	Easter Holiday
30 Apr	Queen's Birthday
4 May	Remembrance Day
5 May	Liberation Day
17 May	Ascension Day
27–28 May	Pentecost/Whitmonday
25–26 Dec	Christmas Holiday

New Zealand
1–2 Jan	New Year's Holiday
22 Jan	Provincial Anniversary (Wellington)
29 Jan	Provincial Anniversary (Auckland)
6 Feb	Waitangi Day
6 Apr	Good Friday
8–9 Apr	Easter Holiday
25 Apr	Anzac Day
4 Jun	Queen's Birthday
22 Oct	Labor Day
16 Nov	Provincial Anniversary (Canterbury)
25 Dec	Christmas
26 Dec	Boxing Day

Norway
1 Jan	New Year's Day
1 Apr	Palm Sunday
5 Apr	Holy Thursday
6 Apr	Good Friday
8–9 Apr	Easter Holiday
1 May	Labor Day
17 May	Ascension Day Constitution Day
27–28 May	Pentecost/Whitmonday
25–26 Dec	Christmas Holiday

Puerto Rico
1 Jan	New Year's Day
6 Jan	Three Kings Day (Epiphany)
8 Jan	Eugenio María de Hostos' Birthday
22 Mar	Emancipation Day
6 Apr	Good Friday
8 Apr	Easter
16 Apr	José de Diego's Birthday
16 Jul	Luis Muñoz Rivera's Birthday
25 Jul	Constitution Day
27 Jul	José Celso Barbosa's Birthday
8 Oct	Día de la Raza
19 Nov	Discovery of Puerto Rico
25 Dec	Christmas
All US federal holidays also observed.

Russia
1–2 Jan	New Year's Holiday
7 Jan	Orthodox Christmas
23 Feb	Soldiers Day
8 Mar	International Women's Day
8 Apr	Orthodox Easter
1–2 May	Spring and Labor Day
9 May	Victory Day
12 Jun	Independence Day
7 Nov	Reconciliation Day
12 Dec	Constitution Day

Singapore
1 Jan	New Year's Day
2 Jan	Hari Raya Haji (Eid-al-Adha)
18–20 Feb	Lunar New Year
6 Apr	Good Friday
8 Apr	Easter
1 May	Labor Day
31 May	Vesak Day (Buddha's Birthday)
9 Aug	National Day
13 Oct	Hari Raya Puasa (Eid-al-Fitr)
9 Nov	Deepavali
20 Dec	Hari Raya Haji (Eid-al-Adha)
25 Dec	Christmas

South Africa
1 Jan	New Year's Day
21 Mar	Human Rights Day
6 Apr	Good Friday
8 Apr	Easter
9 Apr	Family Day
27 Apr	Freedom Day
1 May	Labor Day
16 Jun	Youth Day
9 Aug	National Women's Day
24 Sep	Heritage Day
17 Dec	Day of Reconciliation
25 Dec	Christmas
26 Dec	Day of Goodwill

Spain
1 Jan	New Year's Day
6 Jan	Epiphany
19 Mar	St. Joseph's Day
5 Apr	Holy Thursday
6 Apr	Good Friday
8 Apr	Easter
1 May	Labor Day
25 Jul	St. James the Apostle Day
15 Aug	Assumption Day
12 Oct	National Holiday
1 Nov	All Saints' Day
6 Dec	Constitution Day
8 Dec	Immaculate Conception
25 Dec	Christmas

Switzerland
1 Jan	New Year's Day
2 Jan	Berchtold's Day
6 Apr	Good Friday
8–9 Apr	Easter Holiday
17 May	Ascension Day
27–28 May	Pentecost/Whitmonday
1 Aug	National Day
25 Dec	Christmas
26 Dec	St. Stephen's Day

Thailand
1 Jan	New Year's Day
2 Mar	Makha Bucha Day
6 Apr	Chakri Day
13–15 Apr	Songkran Festival
1 May	Labor Day Visakha Bucha Day (Buddha's Birthday)
7 May	Coronation Day
31 Jul	Buddhist Lent Day
13 Aug	Queen's Birthday
23 Oct	Chulalongkorn Day
5 Dec	King's Birthday
10 Dec	Constitution Day
31 Dec	New Year's Eve

2007

JANUARY

s	m	t	w	t	f	s
	1	2	3	4	5	6
7	8	9	10	11	12	13
14	15	16	17	18	19	20
21	22	23	24	25	26	27
28	29	30	31			

MAY

s	m	t	w	t	f	s
		1	2	3	4	5
6	7	8	9	10	11	12
13	14	15	16	17	18	19
20	21	22	23	24	25	26
27	28	29	30	31		

SEPTEMBER

s	m	t	w	t	f	s
						1
2	3	4	5	6	7	8
9	10	11	12	13	14	15
16	17	18	19	20	21	22
23	24	25	26	27	28	29
30						

FEBRUARY

s	m	t	w	t	f	s
				1	2	3
4	5	6	7	8	9	10
11	12	13	14	15	16	17
18	19	20	21	22	23	24
25	26	27	28			

JUNE

s	m	t	w	t	f	s
					1	2
3	4	5	6	7	8	9
10	11	12	13	14	15	16
17	18	19	20	21	22	23
24	25	26	27	28	29	30

OCTOBER

s	m	t	w	t	f	s
	1	2	3	4	5	6
7	8	9	10	11	12	13
14	15	16	17	18	19	20
21	22	23	24	25	26	27
28	29	30	31			

MARCH

s	m	t	w	t	f	s
				1	2	3
4	5	6	7	8	9	10
11	12	13	14	15	16	17
18	19	20	21	22	23	24
25	26	27	28	29	30	31

JULY

s	m	t	w	t	f	s
1	2	3	4	5	6	7
8	9	10	11	12	13	14
15	16	17	18	19	20	21
22	23	24	25	26	27	28
29	30	31				

NOVEMBER

s	m	t	w	t	f	s
				1	2	3
4	5	6	7	8	9	10
11	12	13	14	15	16	17
18	19	20	21	22	23	24
25	26	27	28	29	30	

APRIL

s	m	t	w	t	f	s
1	2	3	4	5	6	7
8	9	10	11	12	13	14
15	16	17	18	19	20	21
22	23	24	25	26	27	28
29	30					

AUGUST

s	m	t	w	t	f	s
			1	2	3	4
5	6	7	8	9	10	11
12	13	14	15	16	17	18
19	20	21	22	23	24	25
26	27	28	29	30	31	

DECEMBER

s	m	t	w	t	f	s
						1
2	3	4	5	6	7	8
9	10	11	12	13	14	15
16	17	18	19	20	21	22
23	24	25	26	27	28	29
30	31					

2008

JANUARY

s	m	t	w	t	f	s
		1	2	3	4	5
6	7	8	9	10	11	12
13	14	15	16	17	18	19
20	21	22	23	24	25	26
27	28	29	30	31		

FEBRUARY

s	m	t	w	t	f	s
					1	2
3	4	5	6	7	8	9
10	11	12	13	14	15	16
17	18	19	20	21	22	23
24	25	26	27	28	29	

MARCH

s	m	t	w	t	f	s
						1
2	3	4	5	6	7	8
9	10	11	12	13	14	15
16	17	18	19	20	21	22
23	24	25	26	27	28	29
30	31					

APRIL

s	m	t	w	t	f	s
		1	2	3	4	5
6	7	8	9	10	11	12
13	14	15	16	17	18	19
20	21	22	23	24	25	26
27	28	29	30			

MAY

s	m	t	w	t	f	s
				1	2	3
4	5	6	7	8	9	10
11	12	13	14	15	16	17
18	19	20	21	22	23	24
25	26	27	28	29	30	31

JUNE

s	m	t	w	t	f	s
1	2	3	4	5	6	7
8	9	10	11	12	13	14
15	16	17	18	19	20	21
22	23	24	25	26	27	28
29	30					

JULY

s	m	t	w	t	f	s
		1	2	3	4	5
6	7	8	9	10	11	12
13	14	15	16	17	18	19
20	21	22	23	24	25	26
27	28	29	30	31		

AUGUST

s	m	t	w	t	f	s
					1	2
3	4	5	6	7	8	9
10	11	12	13	14	15	16
17	18	19	20	21	22	23
24	25	26	27	28	29	30
31						

SEPTEMBER

s	m	t	w	t	f	s
	1	2	3	4	5	6
7	8	9	10	11	12	13
14	15	16	17	18	19	20
21	22	23	24	25	26	27
28	29	30				

OCTOBER

s	m	t	w	t	f	s
			1	2	3	4
5	6	7	8	9	10	11
12	13	14	15	16	17	18
19	20	21	22	23	24	25
26	27	28	29	30	31	

NOVEMBER

s	m	t	w	t	f	s
						1
2	3	4	5	6	7	8
9	10	11	12	13	14	15
16	17	18	19	20	21	22
23	24	25	26	27	28	29
30						

DECEMBER

s	m	t	w	t	f	s
	1	2	3	4	5	6
7	8	9	10	11	12	13
14	15	16	17	18	19	20
21	22	23	24	25	26	27
28	29	30	31			

NOTES